70.44
7714a

W9-CAE-446

3 5674 05198008 5

CHASE BRANCH LIBRARY
17731 W. SEVEN MILE RD.
DETROIT, MI 48235
578-8002

DEC 2013

CH

Praise for Shari Arison

"Shari, your work has impacted the world in a profoundly positive way, touching lives everywhere in your everlasting pursuit to make the world a better place."

—U.S. President Bill Clinton

"Shari Arison—great wisdom, great capability. The impact is an impact of goodwill of a great spirit. I was deeply impressed by your moving quest to seek out a way to contribute to our world."

—Israeli President Shimon Peres,
Nobel Peace Prize winner

"How did a native New Yorker who grew up in Miami end up the wealthiest woman in the Middle East and one of the most powerful people on the planet? Shari Arison . . . will inspire you, encourage you, and show you how to take your own leap of faith from ordinary to phenomenal."

—Deepak Chopra, M.D., *New York Times* best-selling
author of *Spiritual Solutions*

"I believe that Shari Arison can play a crucial role in our achieving world peace."

—Brian L. Weiss, M.D., *New York Times* best-selling
author of *Many Lives, Many Masters*

Activate
your
Goodness

ALSO BY

Birth: When the Spiritual and
the Material Come Together

Activate your Goodness

TRANSFORMING THE WORLD THROUGH DOING GOOD

Shari Arison

HAY HOUSE, INC.
Carlsbad, California • New York City
London • Sydney • Johannesburg
Vancouver • Hong Kong • New Delhi

Copyright © 2013 by Arison Creative, Ltd.

Published and distributed in the United States by: Hay House, Inc.: www.hayhouse.com® • **Published and distributed in Australia by:** Hay House Australia Pty. Ltd.: www.hayhouse.com.au • **Published and distributed in the United Kingdom by:** Hay House UK, Ltd.: www.hayhouse.co.uk • **Published and distributed in the Republic of South Africa by:** Hay House SA (Pty), Ltd.: www.hayhouse.co.za • **Distributed in Canada by:** Raincoast: www.raincoast.com • **Published in India by:** Hay House Publishers India: www.hayhouse.co.in

Cover design: Karla Baker • *Interior design:* Julie Davison

All rights reserved. No part of this book may be reproduced by any mechanical, photographic, or electronic process, or in the form of a phonographic recording; nor may it be stored in a retrieval system, transmitted, or otherwise be copied for public or private use—other than for "fair use" as brief quotations embodied in articles and reviews—without prior written permission of the publisher.

The author of this book does not dispense medical advice or prescribe the use of any technique as a form of treatment for physical, emotional, or medical problems without the advice of a physician, either directly or indirectly. The intent of the author is only to offer information of a general nature to help you in your quest for emotional and spiritual well-being. In the event you use any of the information in this book for yourself, which is your constitutional right, the author and the publisher assume no responsibility for your actions.

Library of Congress Cataloging-in-Publication Data

Arison, Shari
 Activate your goodness : transforming the world through doing good / Shari Arison. -- 1st ed.
        p. cm.
 ISBN 978-1-4019-3797-3 (hbk. : alk. paper) 1. Conduct of life. 2. Kindness. 3. Humanitarianism. I. Title.
 BJ1589.A75 2013
 170'.44--dc23

                              2012039297

Hardcover ISBN: 978-1-4019-3797-3
Digital ISBN: 978-1-4019-3799-7

16 15 14 13   4 3 2 1
1st edition, March 2013

FSC
www.fsc.org
MIX
Paper from
responsible sources
FSC® C011935

Printed in the United States of America

*This book is dedicated
to every individual who goes
out and does good deeds
for the benefit of others.*

CONTENTS

My Passion
for Doing Good

My name is Shari Arison, and my heart's desire is to inspire people to do good. How did I come to this realization? Well, let's see—when I think about it, it's been a long, hard road.

I was born in America to an Israeli father and a Romanian mother. My mother always said how much she hated the U.S., so as a child, it was very difficult to feel loved by her since I was an American.

Living in New York as a small child, my life back then looked like a scene out the 2011 movie *The Help*, which featured the lives of African-American maids in the South during the early 1960s. Although my parents always treated our housekeeper, Marie, with love and respect, they were both out at work all day, and it was Marie who raised me.

When I was nine years old, we moved to Miami without Marie, which was devastating to me, and then I got another incredible shock when my parents announced they were getting divorced. My mother chose to move to Israel, and my father stayed, seeking the American dream of money and success. As for me, even from a young age, I felt there was something more out there, a deeper connection, and I wondered what exactly it was.

My life drastically changed during this period. I was thrown into a whirlwind of trips back and forth from America to Israel and Israel to America, flying those long distances on my own, making transfers as needed along the way. Imagine a little girl traveling so far by herself. I remember getting lost once in the airport in Amsterdam; it was terrifying.

Thank God that Marie would meet me at the airport in New York. She met me every time and made sure that I found my way through the maze of security and terminals toward my connecting flights. Marie became a lifelong friend to me and to my own children till the day she died. It's a relationship I'll always treasure.

Growing up torn between two worlds—Israel and America—presented tremendous challenges to me. I attended an endless number of schools and always had to make new friends. I was teased in America for being too Israeli, and picked on in Israel for being so American. At that time, the two countries were worlds apart.

In the U.S., homes all had telephones and TVs, but in Israel, you still had to wait seven years to get a phone and TVs were a novelty. Each neighborhood might have only one or two black-and-white TVs, which everyone gathered to watch. The social norms were very far apart as well. As a result, I often felt displaced, disconnected, feeling that the world was cruel, and I must have landed on the wrong planet.

As I grew up, my journey continued with the kinds of ups and downs most people have.

Activate Your Goodness

Although today many think I grew up privileged by wealth, that wasn't the case. My father went bankrupt several times, and he made his fortune after years of hardship. Being a great visionary, and not giving up, he succeeded once he created Carnival Cruise Lines. I was already in my late 20s when success hit and the company went public, although ships were a part of my life from the time we moved to Miami.

So after many years of back and forth, and of serving in the Israeli Army, I settled in Miami for a long haul of 16 years. I married my first husband and had my first three children in the States. Then after years of being a full-time mom, I started our family foundation, the Arison Foundation, and was selected for the board of directors of Carnival. Next came an unfortunate divorce and the Gulf War, where my hours spent in Miami were consumed by worry. I worried terribly about my loved ones in Israel: my mom, aunts, uncles, cousins, and friends. These events put things in perspective for me, and I knew for sure that the place I wanted to be—the place I felt most connected to—was Israel.

By this time, I had already met and married my second husband. Together with my three children, we moved to Israel in the summer of 1991, where my fourth child was born. Once again, it took a while to adjust to a new mentality. I found it was quite different having been a child living in a foreign country, as compared to trying to adjust as a woman and mother to such a different lifestyle and mind-set. Still, I launched a foundation and later a business. I reconnected with family and old friends, and made new ones . . . I was happy and getting on with my life.

But I still faced massive culture shock; even the day-to-day things that we don't think of—such as banking, the rates of exchange on the dollar, the way people communicate or negotiate—were all so different from what I was used to in Miami. Not to mention the chauvinism I experienced for many years as I tried to make it in a male-dominated environment.

Activate Your Goodness

As the years went by, I faced another divorce, another marriage, and yet a third divorce, all along trying to understand myself and the life I was living. I sought out endless techniques, seminars, and lessons and explored myriad doctrines of spirituality. I studied diverse teachings and read many New Age books. I learned and grew . . . and learned and grew.

One lesson was loud and clear: Life dishes out trials and tribulations to all of us. The question is what we do with them.

No matter what I did, I always felt that I was learning my life's lessons the hard way, with a lot of emotional suffering, until one day a few years ago, I just got it. It was like a lightbulb turning on. I felt illuminated: *I want to do good, I want to think good, I want to feel good.*

I was so sick when this insight occurred—physically, emotionally, and spiritually exhausted from a lifetime of fighting. Fighting for what I wanted, whether it was getting attention from my parents as a child or fighting to accomplish my many visions and goals, such as establishing a first-class hospital in Tel Aviv. I worked hard to bring this dream to fruition in order to help our citizens get the best care.

I fought to create an Israeli United Way, which brought in a new culture of giving that is still thriving today. I fought within each of my businesses and philanthropic organizations to implement visionary ideas, such as financial freedom at the bank where I'm a controlling shareholder. Within my infrastructure and real-estate company, I fought to bring in sustainable building practices. I also created a water company with the vision of abundance, which no one could understand at first.

Likewise, it was a struggle to bring about organizations like the Essence of Life, which was founded on the belief that we can only reach world peace by reaching inner peace—each individual within oneself and one's surroundings.

Vision after vision, it was a process of bringing in the right people to create the right teams to

Activate Your Goodness

instill values and set goals that were ahead of their time. Today, there are three universities researching and creating curriculum that is inspired by my values-based business model.

So, yes, these are all beneficial things, personally and professionally satisfying, and I should have been on top of the world. But a couple of years ago, I felt like I was falling apart on all levels, physically, emotionally, and spiritually. I felt that for years, in order for people to understand me, I had to bang my head against the wall. I managed to move a few walls and break a few glass ceilings, but I began to feel overwhelmed, tired, and sick.

When the light came on, I realized that I didn't have to convince anyone, especially those who choose not to see or who don't want to change for whatever reason. If I want to make the world a better place to live in, I could do it by growing the goodness in and around me, and with people who also share that dream.

What a relief it was when I figured out that I didn't have to fight anymore! Today, I just focus on doing my part and connecting to those who want the same as I do: a better world. Do you want a better world?

I have a vision of a good world, a peaceful and happy world, and I say this not because I am naïve and blind. I say this because I *have* been hurt, I *have* had trials and tribulations, but I *believe* that things can be different.

I've learned from my past experiences, and I continue to learn every day. But I now believe that these life lessons can be gained without suffering. I have faith that we can create the healthy, positive environment we want for ourselves, our children, and our planet.

I try to uphold this within everything that I do, both personally and in my business and philanthropic group. So it was with this in mind that I took my passion and belief in the power of doing good, and initiated Good Deeds Day in Israel in 2007. It started out as a simple idea: For one day,

Activate Your Goodness

each person would do something good for someone else or for the world. We started out with a few thousand people, including my family and my employees, and it's been growing every year to where it has now crossed borders and has become an international day of doing good.

Every year on Good Deeds Day, I personally go out to do my good deed, traveling all over the place. It's such a delight to witness the numerous individual and collective acts of goodness springing up. At each place I visit, I'm so touched, and my heart is filled with all the goodness that I see. I ask myself, *Wouldn't it be wonderful if every day were like this?* It can be. I truly believe it can be so.

We all have a part to play in achieving this. That's why we at Arison keep expanding our efforts each year, to make more and more people aware of the *power of doing good.* We want to encourage every man, woman, and child to express their goodness not only on this one day, but every day . . . in every moment of their lives.

This book is my way to explain how all this "doing good" works, how you can make it work for yourself and activate your own goodness. It starts by loving and respecting yourself, and then that positive energy ripples out to the world, transforming everything along the way.

◊　　　◊　　　◊

CHAPTER ONE

Calling All
to Do Good

Imagine how it would feel if you woke up one morning with a certainty in your heart—indeed, a certainty that had been there your whole life— that a huge shift was coming? That this change was needed and wanted and inevitable . . . that it would eventually permeate the whole world?

I've always wished for this change. We're all part of it, everyone in the world. We all have a stake in our collective future. We have a choice to make—to take responsibility here and now—on how we conduct ourselves, with our own selves and with others, and to fully realize how our choices impact our surroundings, our planet, and all of humanity.

All my life I wondered, *What is my role?* I explored this both within myself and with the help of others. Since we all have to take personal responsibility, I began by asking myself, *What can I offer to the world, given my specific skills, life experiences, and through the platforms that I will attain?*

I've worked since my teenage years and entered the family business in my early 20s in Miami when it was just taking off. Fast-forward to today: We live in Israel, my youngest son is completing high school, and my global business and philanthropic interests are headquartered here. So to be part of this shift, I felt (and I still feel) the need to start with myself, since this is an ongoing process, and then reach out within my own circles.

In addition to my skills, I knew I could draw on my life experiences as well. As I mentioned, I've lived through all kinds of ups and downs, and they didn't break me. I talked more in detail about all those life challenges in my first book, called *Birth:*

When the Spiritual and the Material Come Together, so enough said on all that. But as I reflect back on my life, I feel blessed by all I have, all that I have lived through—the good and the bad times—for they have made me who I am today. I'm more determined than ever to take personal responsibility for my part in improving our world. When I was asked to write a second book, I said yes and decided to make it about the power of "doing good." I knew that in this book, I could include my experiences of promoting the idea of doing good as an individual and within my companies and organizations. I want to inspire people with this concept, knowing that everyone is capable of making a huge difference.

This is a simple and universal vision—one that I live with passion. The concept of *doing good* came to me a few years ago, when a light came on in the darkness. These two words sum up so much of what I've always believed, and when I began to introduce this concept to the people around me, they felt inspired, too. I soon saw that I was on to something.

Activate Your Goodness

This vision is based on the belief that by doing good; thinking good; and consciously choosing to use positive words, feelings, and actions every day, each of us can enhance the goodness in our world. I believe that the time has come for this vision to manifest within all of us, in all corners of the world.

Doing Good Is Good Business

Even before this vision of doing good became really clear to me, I've worked my whole life to create change within myself, my surroundings, and within the Arison Group of business and philanthropic organizations. Certainly, from the beginning, the Arison Foundation has been professionally run in the same way as all of our business units. We listen to the needs of the communities here in Israel and we understand that we're not just giving funds to charities, but we're also choosing to make important social investments in our collective future.

For several years now, all our business and philanthropic entities have been implementing long-term visions and instilling values. And now I can say that we're proving that *doing good is good business.* It's a whole new way of doing business that many companies are waking up to.

But *Activate Your Goodness* is not so much about companies and organizations. The reason for this book is that I believe that all this good starts with each of us as an individual. This is the journey I'd like you to consider taking along with me—it's a personal challenge. It's based on a very simple premise: *All you have to do is think good, speak good, and do good.* This is my main goal, and I'm so fortunate to have so many employees worldwide who have come together in helping to implement this change in mind-set and show the world it can be done.

So you wouldn't be alone in this journey—far from it! The Arison Group has already engaged our own large global workforce, more than 24,000 employees who are working within the vision of doing good. Our collective efforts also helped encourage more than 250,000 people in Israel and thousands more around the globe to "activate their goodness"—by doing a good deed on our annual Good Deeds Day in 2012.

Could it really be this simple? Think good, speak good, do good? Well, yes and no. If it were this easy, why are we at war with each other? Why is there so much suffering? Why are there still so many rude and aggressive people? Why were you cut off in traffic this morning?

The way I see it, there are two paths we can choose to take. One leads to further conflict, and the other takes us toward greater compassion and peace. In the first case, we see that conflict is on the rise; and with it comes deeper economic crises, ongoing wars and famines, more unemployment, heightened levels of global warming . . . you name it.

But at the same time, I look around and see love and compassion. More and more people give of themselves these days than before, and greater numbers of individuals take action and partner with others to make the world a better place to live in. I see countless people who care deeply about their fellow human beings, animals, and the environment. I believe that on a whole, we're becoming tired of negativity, and we're consciously looking to find ways to effect positive change.

The Power of Doing Good

Love and compassion are alive. Just imagine if everyone could come onboard! If each person in the world could just remember to consciously think good, speak good, and do good, I believe we can transform ourselves, and through that process, we'll collectively transform the world.

So this book is about "doing good"—which seems pretty simple and straightforward. But do you know how to give from a genuinely positive place and how to graciously receive? Are you kind to yourself first? That's the first step, and one I struggled with for many years.

Activate Your Goodness

For the most part, our concepts of good and bad, and the rules of life, were learned as children growing up. For me, that was first in New York, and then in Miami and Israel. My family is Jewish, but we lived a secular lifestyle; even so, from the time I was very young, I personally felt extremely Jewish and had a deep connection to Israel.

Today, people say to me that I'm more religious than "the religious," but I prefer to think of myself as spiritual. I am a spiritual being—as we all are—on a quest to find our true passion and path. I strive to live my life fully and authentically in both the material and spiritual realms. I feel a great passion to help all of humanity, and my path is to inspire a change in people to do good.

The time is now, because we need to replace the old patterns of human behavior and society that were very much based on scarcity, greed, and fear. I'm proposing that collectively we have the power to replace those old beliefs that aren't working anymore through doing good, and I'm asking each person in the world to connect to this vision and contribute to it. For it to truly work, we need a critical mass of people to step up and join in.

The beautiful thing about doing good is that it doesn't matter where you live, where you go to school, or what you do for a living; it doesn't even matter how old you are or what cultural group you belong to. Any and every single person can make extraordinary things happen when they use the power of doing good, first for themselves and then letting it ripple out into the world.

From what I can see, many people around the world have been yearning for change over the past few years, and have begun to seek out greater meaning and depth in their lives. I know I have, too. The countless men and women I meet in my daily life, the authors I read, the leaders I respect— from all over the world—seem to be experiencing this phase of change and are beginning to shed outdated patterns and liberate themselves from the old by moving on to the new.

Activate Your Goodness

In Search of Authenticity

In order for a monumental change to actually take place, a critical mass is required, driven by the energy of goodness and authentic goodwill. Only when an enormous number of people think good, speak good, and do good can we generate an essential and lasting change in the state of humankind.

What I see happening is this: As more and more of us discover and express our authentic selves, we create a new reality that emphasizes new values—values based on unity, love, friendship, and compassion. Most of all, we develop the capacity of universal acceptance, which is the ability to accept ourselves and others, despite our differences.

Each of us can use our unique talents to effect this change, and you can make an impact in any field that you're in. Since I'm a businessperson and I have a strong moral compass, many of my activities revolve around business and philanthropy, but I strive just as hard to do good in my personal life and day-to-day relationships. Things don't always go perfectly—because none of us is perfect—but every day, I am trying.

Here at Arison, we're finding that through thoughtful business leadership, we are creating a better world. This is because business and philanthropic initiatives (unlike countries) have no borders, and the affect we can have is worldwide.

And while I am highly spiritual, I am just as equally practical. As I mentioned, the Arison Group includes philanthropic organizations and businesses. Our businesses are both public and private in the fields of finance, real estate, infrastructure, salt, water, and energy. In business, we look first and foremost at the economic aspect of everything we do. But as we examine all the aspects of each business deal, we sometimes discover that it may have negative consequences to people or the planet, and in those cases, we won't go forward with it because, in the long term, we won't derive a profit.

Activate Your Goodness

Money in itself isn't sufficient to be our sole driving force; we see this very clearly today. On the other hand, when we select projects and initiatives that sustain the world, we sustain ourselves as an enterprise. When the world profits, then we profit, too. Without a doubt, doing good *is* good business.

Leading an authentic life and learning to give and receive in balance aren't the easiest things in the world to do. Good deeds sometimes go awry, and well-meaning intentions fall short. It's not a straight line, but I believe that doing good has the power not only to transform your life and enrich you greatly, but it also has the power to cause a ripple effect that will be felt around the world. Our personal and collective acts of kindness to ourselves and others will ultimately impact all aspects of life, the planet, and the whole of humanity.

That's a pretty big challenge, I realize, so let's start by doing good for the most important person in the world first: *you!*

CHAPTER TWO

Doing Good for Yourself

When a flight attendant on an airplane instructs you about what to do in case of an emergency, he or she always tells you to put the oxygen mask on yourself before you put it on your children or anyone else who needs assistance. This sounds almost absurd at first, as the natural reaction of any parent would be to immediately help their child. Yet if you don't care for yourself first, you won't be able to care for anyone else. You must help yourself, or you will be of no help to anyone else.

It seems simple when explained in this way, but being good to yourself every day, being loving

Activate Your Goodness

and compassionate to yourself on a consistent basis, isn't really so simple. There are so many reasons why people don't love themselves and why they continue to put the needs or wants of others before their own, even to the detriment of their own health and well-being.

You may be one of these overly kind souls. Perhaps you're one of the many who was taught by your parents that you should always give to others before yourself because giving to yourself is self-ish. Many religious teachings are about service to others and giving to the needy. But I believe that if you don't take care of yourself first, you'll simply have nothing left to give!

Doing good for yourself starts with loving your-self, and that means accepting and loving who you are at any given moment. In order to do this, you first need to get to know yourself. You're probably think-ing, *I know myself!* But do you really? Do you know what you truly want and what makes you feel good? Do you know how to listen to yourself, your body, your soul? Do you treat your body as the temple it is, giving it the best nutrition and plenty of rest? Are you genuinely happy, healthy, and at peace?

Few of us have reached this point of pure balance because our lives are so hectic and filled with too much stimulation. We all need to cope with our ongoing challenges, but are we dealing with our daily lives in a positive and healthy way? So many of us work too hard, get too little rest, don't exercise enough, shop too much, and spend too much time on the computer. And some take it to the extreme by excessively smoking, drinking, eating, or even doing drugs. Too much of anything throws us off balance and keeps us from being truly content within ourselves.

Like many others, I've struggled with my weight at different times throughout my life—overeating, not exercising enough—and had a hard time getting myself back on track. So I do understand. It's not easy to overcome these things and find balance, but you can do it.

Nobody wants to be overweight, overworked, or addicted to drugs. No one wants to feel unhappy or stressed out. These are symptoms of something much deeper that's going on inside oneself. As human beings, over the years we've accumulated layers upon layers of hurts, fears, frustrations, and anger. But underneath all of this is our authentic self, an individual worthy of love and acceptance. Our essence is like a diamond, but when we're covered by layers of "dirt" and negative energy, those layers conceal our true self.

Developing Self-Awareness Through Introspection

There are many ways to shed the layers of negative energy. I've spoken about this at length in my first book, and there are countless self-help and New Age books with different techniques you might try. I've personally found that the best place to start is to take a good look at myself. Introspection works; it isn't quick or easy, but it's effective. When you learn to see and love yourself for who you are, when you're connected to what you truly want, doing good for yourself will become second nature.

The first step is self-awareness, so be as honest as you can with yourself. Don't judge or blame yourself or anyone else for your perceived faults or shortcomings. No excuses. Then ask yourself, *How do I feel?* Let your feelings come up and out in a positive way. Once you're cleansed, you can look more deeply at what you truly want in life.

I understand how hard this is to do. Many times I've said, "I'll start my diet tomorrow," and never followed through. And many times I've heard friends say, "I'm going to quit smoking," but they couldn't. It's okay. Just keep cleansing the layers that are hindering you from making positive choices. Keep focused on what you desire and ask in your heart a pure intention to someone higher than yourself. I would say God; another person would say a Higher Power or the Universe. Choose what's right for you. Just remember to ask for something good.

Here are some examples of using the process of introspection. One is to sit quietly, focusing on

Activate Your Goodness

your breath, quieting your brain, and just letting your feelings rise up in your body. Keep breathing deeply, focusing on each breath, and ask yourself, *What is it that I feel?* Become aware of your feelings, really feel those emotions, and then release them, through crying, screaming, or even writing them down in a journal . . . whatever method works for you. The main point is to acknowledge it and then let it go, cleansing yourself of the layers of energy you've been holding on to. But remember, this is a process for yourself, by yourself. Don't take it out on anyone else.

Another introspective technique is to look at yourself in a mirror. Deeply gaze into your eyes. What are they telling you? Are they sad? If you see sadness, make a conscious choice for happiness. It might feel uncomfortable at first, but stick with it. Just remain focused, breathe deeply, look deeply, and listen to what your soul is telling you. Be patient. With a little practice, the answers will come.

What I have found is that when you truly love and accept yourself just as you are, you'll start to make better life choices. You'll set healthy boundaries to protect yourself from the negativity in your environment, you'll begin to feel more compassion for others, and your love will ripple out to the world in wondrous ways.

As you shed the energy you no longer need, layer by layer, it's just like cleansing the layers of dirt that cover your inner diamond, and your true essence shines through. It's not usually one cleansing, but many, since quite likely it has taken years to build up the layers that hinder you. Just when you think you're done, you may find more layers coming to the surface. That happened with me, and now I can accept that introspection and cleansing of energy have become part of my daily routine.

As you go through this process of introspection, you might discover things that you don't like about yourself, but don't fight against them. That will just cause resistance. Force brings more force.

Activate Your Goodness

Therefore, accept all the things that arise, whether you like them or not. It's only when you accept them can you then release them.

Discover What Works for You

If these techniques are challenging for you, there are other ways that can help you uncover your true self. Don't be afraid to ask for help. I've explored many techniques over the years along my journey to release the layers of energy that built up in my body and soul. Taking time for your personal development isn't indulgent, selfish, or self-serving. Rather, it is necessary and vital to be good to yourself, if you wish to do good for others.

What happens when you try these techniques and become more aware of yourself is that you'll be able to let go of what you no longer need. For example, if you're holding on to anger, the anger is an energy that is within and around you. Most people think that a certain emotion is part of who they are, but I don't believe that to be so. Anger, or any other emotion, is just energy. We know that we don't want to feel angry, for instance, but it's very difficult at times to see the difference between the anger and who we are at our core.

However, the process of cleansing and self-discovery results in self-awareness, and with greater self-awareness, you'll see that you don't need that anger or the past hurts anymore. You don't need those aspects of yourself that you've struggled with; they don't work for goodness, and they're not who you are. You are pure love at your core, at your essence—we all are. Once you let go of the clouds of hurtful things and painful emotions, you will find that you *can* choose good.

So in practical terms, when negative thoughts arise, become conscious of those thoughts and focus instead on what you want in a healthy manner. For example, maybe you're mad at yourself because you stayed up too late the night before and you woke up exhausted. Instead of beating yourself up, train your thoughts to respond in a loving way. Think instead, *I want to create a better day.*

Activate Your Goodness

Don't be hard on yourself if you find you have endless negative thinking; just keep trying to focus on good thoughts. It's like training your body to be in shape. At first, when you start a new exercise program, you can hardly breathe and each new activity is exhausting. But as you stick with it, it soon becomes easier and easier. In the same way, you'll have to expend some effort to consistently focus on good thoughts, but with practice, it will come more easily and naturally.

At the same time, pay attention to the words that come out of your mouth. Do your words make you feel good or bad about yourself? Try to consciously speak out loud in a loving way. With practice, this too will become easier.

In addition to thinking good and speaking good, take action. As you begin to feel better and get rid of the layers that are holding you back, you'll naturally have thoughts of all the good things you can do that are healthy for your body and mind. Now is the time to take action!

Take Action for Yourself

Notice what makes you happy, what fills you full of energy, and what makes your body tingle. Once you know, do what makes you thrive. Perhaps you love to write, create works of art, or cook. But with all your day-to-day responsibilities, you think, *I just don't have time for those things anymore.*

It's necessary to make time for the things you love. It's good to dance, laugh, or create art—activities like these feed your soul and can be very soothing and relaxing. Running each morning just for the joy of it, watching a funny movie with a friend, tending the garden and watching things grow, petting your dog each morning when you wake up . . . when you take any kind of concrete action that is positive for you, it will make you feel better and fill you with light.

For me, I started noticing over the years that I felt drained whenever I had to participate in activities I didn't really enjoy or when I was around certain people. I just didn't feel good, and it was

Activate Your Goodness

exhausting. When I became more aware, more in touch with my authentic self, I paid attention to what was uplifting to me and what was draining. I now choose to go to places and be with individuals who make me feel good.

I also made a conscious choice to use my free time to do things that I truly enjoy. For me, that's going to the beach, watching a movie, reading a book, meditating, or expressing my creativity through sculpting, drawing, or dancing. When you choose to do things that are uplifting for you, you'll have more positive energy for all aspects of your life.

Through introspection, I also realized that I'm the type of person who needs to have time by myself to recharge. I might listen to music, take a walk, or just sit quietly and enjoy the solitude. Once I started to consciously add these quiet times into my days, it made a big difference. I still have a busy schedule, but I have more energy for it because I consistently take time for personal reflection and to recharge.

Getting to know yourself and what makes you feel good is so important. It's relatively easy to add a few simple things to your day. Remember, when you think good, speak good, and do good, you transform yourself inside; and by doing so, you transform the world. Our next step together is to apply these principles outward and allow the good inside of you to ripple out to those who are closest to you, in your immediate circle of life.

◊　　　◊　　　◊

CHAPTER THREE

Doing Good
for Those
Closest to You

Whether we know it or not, our energy creates a ripple effect like a stone that's thrown into the ocean. We all have a vibration that resonates within us and out into the world. The first circle outside ourselves where this ripple effect is felt is within our homes. Goodness has the power to soothe and delight the ones we care most about; it is contagious. But so is the ripple effect caused by negative energy. If we choose to bring a cloud of bad energy home with us, guess what? Everyone in the house quickly becomes infected.

Activate Your Goodness

Just imagine a man coming home from work, fuming mad about something that happened to him that day. He slams the car door, tears through the front door, and stomps off past his wife, without so much as a hello. She was probably looking forward to his return home, but now she's worried and anxious. Did he lose his job? Is he mad at her for some reason? She sits at the table, feeling sad and frightened. It's a scene that could happen in any home. You know what it's like.

But—wait—what if we did a rewind and played the scene again? This time the same man comes home from work, fuming mad about something that happened to him that day, and he slams the car door as he gets out. He stomps up the walkway to the front door, but he catches himself just before he enters the house. The man realizes that his anger is at the boiling point, and it's about to enter his home with him.

He pauses and makes a conscious effort to calm down first. He takes a few deep breaths and blows them out—releasing the angry emotions with each

28

exhale. He knows that his anger had nothing to do with his family, and besides, now he's at home.

The deep breaths soothe his nerves, and he's able to enter the house calmly. He takes off his coat and greets his wife with a warm smile, bending down to give her a hug where she's sitting. She smiles back, points out to him something funny that she was looking at online on her laptop, and they share a laugh together. What a much more pleasant way to begin their evening together.

Quite a different scenario! How powerful the change was when the man realized his anger, and it took less than a minute to calm himself down. It was just a few deep breaths, but *he made the choice to think good.* Then he *spoke good*—a warm greeting to his wife. He followed that by *doing good.* He took a moment to hug her and listen to her news about her day.

He was quite likely still somewhat upset, but he didn't let that cloud of negative energy enter his house and affect his loved ones. Plus he felt better himself because he was able to enjoy his family, eating dinner together and relaxing without having caused an unpleasant scene. This is the power of doing good, and it's a great example of how easy it is to do.

Perhaps later on, the man and his wife had a quiet conversation about their day where he could tell her why he was so upset, but by then they'll both be calmer and better able to handle it. Quite often, after we calm down, we can see even the most upsetting events in a different light.

Choosing Harmony Instead of Chaos

This awareness and acceptance can be done any time you feel angry, upset, frustrated, or sad. Your emotions may be intense, but they're just fields of energy. You are the one who can choose how they'll affect you: they can ruin your day completely, or you can choose to look at them and release them in a positive way.

But what if it's someone close to you in your immediate family who is driving you crazy? You can't exactly throw them out or move, because this person is important to you. And you can't change someone else; you can only change yourself. It is totally up to the other person to decide to change or not. It's that way in nature, too—a bird is a bird and a fish is a fish. A bird cannot change the fish into a bird, nor can a fish change the bird into a fish. But we humans assume that we can change each other, and it can cause endless grief within families. Well, it might have seemed endless until now.

So before an argument with a loved one gets completely out of hand, quiet yourself and say (even just inside your head): *I choose calm.* Sounds simple, right? But if it were that easy, why doesn't everyone do it? What I've realized is that when someone upsets me, it's really a trigger to show me something within myself. If I'm angry at someone, the anger is really an energy that's within me. So I ask myself, *What has this outburst triggered within me? What do I need to resolve in order to feel better?* Once I look at the anger within myself and understand it, I can then release it, breathe deeply, and choose calm.

When we acknowledge that we're all covered-up diamonds—and we know the process that it takes to uncover our layers and come to accept and love ourselves—we can then accept others with greater awareness and compassion. We can also learn to be thankful to them for showing us what we need to resolve within ourselves.

It helps to remember that our loved ones are worthy of compassion just as we are. They've had their own set of hurts, frustrations, and disappointments; and they're likely reacting from a place of fear and pain. Give them the benefit of the doubt and try to meet them halfway—to understand their point of view and extend love to them.

Many family upsets come about because someone wants to change the other person. Each person feels that their way is the right way, and everyone else should agree. But you have to accept that those you love are different from you; after all, each person in the world is unique.

They may want different things, but they're still your family.

When we accept this rule of nature, "You can't change someone else," and we choose to give up fixating on changing other people and convincing them of our own views, we officially have permission to let go. We can still offer support, encouragement, and understanding. We can offer to pay for therapy, rehab, or career counseling—whatever might help them—but in the end, those we're trying to help have to want it, or it simply isn't going to work.

In this case, just keep on loving them. Love yourself with all your heart, and love them just as intensely. See the good inside them at their core; see their essence, the diamond that may be covered up. Think good thoughts about them, and speak well of them. Believe in them. Take positive actions, but don't impose your will. This is all that you can do, but it's powerful. More powerful than yelling—that's for sure.

Activate Your Goodness

Regretfully, though, as powerful as doing good is, it doesn't always work. Different times over the years, I've had situations in my life where I've tried and tried to be positive and do everything in my power to resonate positive thoughts toward specific people in my life. But sometimes, no matter what you do, that other person might still choose to be enveloped in their own negativity or anger, and holding on to their past upsets.

Accepting and Letting Go

Eventually, you'll realize that you just have to accept that this is the way someone is, and no amount of positive thinking or loving thoughts or actions from you will be able to change them. At that point, you may have to accept that this person may never change, and if so, you cannot remain together or even stay in touch. What I found is that situations like this are just not healthy for me, since I couldn't be happy in that kind of environment.

Whenever you have to let go of and separate from a person whom you've loved deeply—whether it be a spouse, parent, child, sibling, or a dear friend—there are going to be painful feelings that arise, such as anger, hurt, betrayal, blame, guilt, disappointment, and others. As hard as it can be, you have to really look at these painful emotions, allow yourself to feel them, and then let them go in a positive way. Keep a loving, open heart. If you want to do good for yourself and others, let go with love. You never know what tomorrow will bring.

The process of letting go and how you deal with it is completely up to you. Just remember, it's not selfish to choose good for yourself; it's necessary, and you have the responsibility to choose the best situation for yourself and others. Not all interpersonal relationships work out. Yet most times, I've found that when I choose good and resonate goodness out to those close to me, it does effect a positive change.

Activate Your Goodness

The power of doing good and sharing healthy emotions with those around you has been proven. Loving gestures, warm hugs, and a happy smile— these are all things that even the youngest children can understand. In fact, I recently saw a show on TV that illustrated this in quite an amazing way.

On this program, there were several small children in a room with large cushiony dolls that were seated around them. The children were watching a show on TV—a show with scenes where a range of different people, of all ages and sizes, were giving friendly hugs to each other, generally showing warmth and affection. Almost immediately, the children in the room began to hug the dolls that were with them. They quickly picked up on what to do, mimicking what they had seen.

Then as I continued to watch, the same sort of experiment was duplicated, but this time, the program that the children were exposed to showed people of all ages hitting and punching each other. Almost immediately, the children began to mimic what they saw and started to hit and punch the dolls in the same way they had witnessed on the second show.

It was quite amazing to see this experiment play out in these two dramatic ways. It reminded me of how important it is to be kind at all times; you don't know who will be watching or what they will pick up from your behavior. The more you practice doing good for yourself and for your loved ones, the more it will become a way of life that encompasses all of that and much more.

The simple power that is present in a hug and a smile has been proven in many ways. When I watched the TV show where the children hugged the dolls, it brought such warmth to my heart and soul. It reminded me of a story I heard when we were getting so many personal testimonials about Good Deeds Day in Israel.

The Power of Positive Energy

This story came from the offices of Dr. Blum, when he was the head of the neurology department in one of the top hospitals in Israel. His office actually looked more like a child's room than a doctor's office. Dozens of brightly colored teddy bears were scattered around on every table, chair, and shelf—even on his examination table.

"Here in the department they call me Dr. Teddy Bear," he would say with a grin. Dr. Blum laughs and smiles a lot. "Laughing is very healthy," he pointed out. "In general, our mood, our emotional situation, and our spiritual energy level all have a tremendous effect on our recovery. That's what I learned when I decided to study complementary medicine in addition to conventional medicine."

But the teddy bears, he admits, were an idea from his youngest daughter, 16-year-old Maya. "We talk a lot about my work in the hospital because she's very interested in the topic and is thinking about studying medicine. One day she asked what was the most difficult stage in treating patients, and without having to think twice, I immediately replied that it was recuperation.

"There are many cases in which the treatment succeeds beyond expectations, but the patient has a slow and very difficult recuperation," Dr. Blum went on to explain. "Together, we tried to think of how we could assist in their recovery, and Maya said, 'We need to find a way to give them recovery energy that will stay with them for a long time.' She suggested that we 'charge' the teddy bears with positive energy and then give them to the patients."

That's how the "recovery bears" project was born. "Maya had a huge collection of teddy bears, and she decided to donate all of them to the project," Dr. Blum recalls. "We sat and meditated together, and transferred good recuperative energy to the bears. Then we gave them out at the hospital."

Dr. Blum says the response was astounding. Patients who got the bears reported a decrease in anxiety levels, a deeper and more peaceful sleep, and a speedier recovery. "Other people heard about the 'recovery bears' and wanted to help, so they started to donate bears, and today we can give a 'recovery bear' fully charged with positive recuperative energy to every patient in the hospital," says the man who is proud to be known as Dr. Teddy Bear.

When you look at it, this was a simple enough experiment, and it worked! One family, Dr. Blum and his daughter, proved that goodwill and positive energy have the power to transform those touched by that goodness. As you travel your own path of goodness, you will begin to fully realize your own potential, too.

You'll be much better able to support your loved ones while they're on their own journey toward reaching their potential. Before long, you will find that doing good permeates every aspect of your life, enriching yourself and your loved ones, bringing your family members increased vitality and joy.

It's Never Too Late for Healing

I'm constantly amazed by the power of doing good. I had cause to realize this power even more so, when in recent years, I witnessed both my parents suffer with illness and pass away. In 1999, I lost my father, Ted Arison, to cancer, heart disease, and diabetes; in 2012, my mother, Mina Arison Sapir, passed away of chronic lung disease.

They were both living in Israel, close to me and my family during these times. I found myself on two different periods, sitting first next to my father, then years later with my mother, waiting on doctors' reports and test results, dealing with frightful scares of them being rushed to the hospital, jumping at every phone call, and the agony of watching someone you love suffering so much.

As stressful as all this was for them and for me, I was thankful that I was able to be there to support them. Throughout our lives, I didn't have the warmest and closest of bonds with my mom and dad; I think because of the culture they grew up in, they weren't the type to show deep emotion or affection. When I was growing up and for most of my life with them, emotions were kept tightly wrapped. But despite our differences, I respected and loved them, and I know they loved me.

Activate Your Goodness

That's why I consider it a blessing that later in our lives, we were able to overcome the hurt, anger, miscommunications, and disappointments of the past and found ourselves able to forgive. I was fortunate to have been given the chance to say everything that was in my heart before they passed away. I feel blessed that I was able to listen to them, show them who I truly was, and finally have a real, deeply connected relationship, even if it was only near the end.

My father specifically requested not to have a eulogy after his death; however, at my mother's funeral, I chose to give a eulogy. I spoke about her many strengths and good qualities, and also reflected upon the ups and downs and the reality of our lives. I spoke about how after years of being distant, we came to a point where a genuine sense of togetherness was created—a family bond was formed, one that was warm and loving.

I said at her funeral that this shows it is never too late. It's never too late to talk, to listen, to understand, and to accept each other. It's never too late to forgive. It wasn't an easy speech to deliver at such an emotional time, but I felt compelled to share our complicated journey with our friends and families that day.

I was glad I did! It turned out that by sharing so honestly, I received incredible feedback from those who attended. Even weeks and months later, I heard from people who were so touched by the goodness within our story that they felt inspired to reach out and resolve some long-standing hurts within their own families.

Just as I've said from the very beginning, when you think good, speak good, and do good, you transform yourself inside. And by doing so, your goodness ripples out to the people around you.

Let's take this principle to the next level: to your neighbors, classmates, co-workers, and anyone else you come into contact with each day. The effect of your goodness is felt by everyone you meet.

◊   ◊   ◊

CHAPTER FOUR

Doing Good in
Your Daily Life

As we grow and proceed through our daily lives, we're all seeking our place in the world. It's a process to find our path and discover our true calling. Yet I believe that through doing good, we can absolutely accomplish this.

In many ways, life is like an orchestra. Each instrument is unique, with its own frequency, tone, pitch, and sound. The cello is a cello, the piano is a piano, the violin is a violin . . . each and every instrument has its own unique voice, which must be carefully tuned on a regular basis.

Then the musicians must respect each other throughout the piece, letting each instrument play its proper role. When instruments are in tune and played with respect for the others, beautiful music is produced by the orchestra. But if the instruments are not perfectly tuned or played in respectful unison, the result is simply noise.

We can learn from the musician who tunes the instrument quietly first, before joining the orchestra. I believe that in our daily lives, we must tune our inner self before we sound it out to others, so we can make sure our voice and emotions are clear, correct, and genuine—that we are playing our own authentic notes.

Once we're in tune with ourselves, just like the musicians, we must be mindful of the other people around us, respecting their individuality and beliefs in order for harmony to reign. On the other hand, if we don't keep ourselves in tune, and we don't treat others with respect, there will be nothing but noise and chaos within our daily environments, be it at work, at school, or at home.

In this way, it's up to us to choose to create chaos or harmony in our lives. Which notes do you choose to hear? Do you choose a harsh tune of anger and hatred or a soft tune of love and compassion? Strive to really listen and send out a personal tune that is precise, beautiful, and respectful—one that can change the atmosphere in your daily life from noise to music, from chaos to harmony.

I believe that our search for a harmonious world begins and ends with doing good. Goodness pours out of us in ever-expanding circles, reaching beyond ourselves and our homes to our neighbors, classmates, co-workers, and all those individuals we come in contact with each day.

As you go about your daily activities, be aware that doing good is not only the giving of material things. There are many and varied ways to do good for yourself and for those around you. A smile, a kind word, thoughtful advice, a supportive shoulder, a listening ear—none of these acts cost the giver anything, but they are likely to be worth much more to the recipient than you can imagine.

I believe that we're all born with goodness inside us, and we soon learn from our parents about good and bad. As a child, I wanted to do good and sensed a lot of wrongs in the world. I couldn't figure out how people could be so cruel. Even in the schoolyard, I couldn't understand why all the children didn't get along with each other. Sure enough, throughout my life I continued to have these concerns, and I still do. We don't live in a perfect world, and inside ourselves, there's a constant struggle, too. Good or bad—it is our choice.

Discovering What You Have to Offer

By choosing to do good, you can find your place in life. Here's one of the ways it worked for me. When I first started to serve on the board of one of my companies in Israel many years ago, I felt very self-conscious. My background was in the leisure and travel business, which I loved, and I ran a small business and my family's foundation as well. However, I was like a fish out of water when surrounded at the table by so many financial people.

At first, I compared myself to everyone else on the board who were highly skilled in finance and who were all about the numbers. It took me a while, and I tried to fit in, but I finally realized that I shouldn't compare myself to them. When they went through the financial statements, I was bored, but they came alive.

But then, when it came to talking about vision and strategy, about caring for the customer and branding, and about giving back to the community, that's when *I* came alive! I had so much to offer; I was thrilled to find my place in that environment. And when I started to really get into these things and talked about vision, most of the other people at the table didn't understand the importance of vision and values.

That's when I realized I didn't need to be like them. What I had to offer was very different from what they had to offer, but it was still a critical part of the overall picture. That's when I understood that each of us has a place where we can use our own unique talents for the greater good. Life is like

Activate Your Goodness

a big puzzle that we are each a part of. Each puzzle piece is unique in size, shape, and color. You can't tell what the puzzle is of, until you see all the pieces placed together and the full image appears!

Like those colorful puzzle pieces, everyone's life is different. My life at work happens to revolve around business and philanthropic enterprises, which I balance with family time and my personal life. Other people may work as miners or chefs, farmers or teachers, scientists or students; or they may be employed in retail, health care, or work at home as parents or care providers—the list of careers and life paths to choose in this world is endless.

There are many ways to discover your unique talents and your own life path, but why not start with doing good? Try to think outside the box to find where you fit in. Not everyone who is musically talented is obliged to be a concert musician, especially if they happen to suffer from stage fright. But they could certainly become a music teacher, for example.

How Do You Wish to Be Seen?

As you set out to find your own purpose, think about the many encounters you have during your daily routines. Look closely at the image this reflects back at you: Is this how you wish to be seen in the eyes of the world? Is this what you wish to see in the world? If not, you should review your choices and see what might need to be corrected so you're living up to the potential you have at your core.

I believe you too can find your true passion and talent; your place in the orchestra of life. Your passion and talents are not so much connected to your education as they are to your choices. You have the ultimate choice as to how you're seen within your world of work and within your daily activities. Ask yourself, *What do I feel most excited about? What makes me feel like I'm growing as a person? Where do I want my life path to go?*

Through your daily life, you have a wonderful opportunity to discover ways to fully develop

Activate Your Goodness

your passions and talents. When you find a path you love, you can live, study, or work with a feeling of being fulfilled; it is something to strive for. And I believe that doing good is a way to add extra value to all aspects of your life, and it can guide you toward goals that are greater than you are. When you consistently choose to think good, speak good, and do good, all aspects of your daily life will be enhanced.

For me in my daily life, I've been able to integrate doing good in my home life and throughout all of my businesses and philanthropic endeavors. I enjoy being able to inspire others through these activities and model to people how taking action and doing good can really make a huge difference in our world.

So many people choose to take positive action. One story I particularly loved was about Keren, who was employed by a big high-tech company. She worked very long hours, and during the week, she dedicated herself completely to her work.

But on the weekends, Keren would turn to her special project: dream cakes. "Since I was a child, I've always loved baking," she said. "But in recent years, I'd realized that I was making more cakes than my family and friends could eat. Everyone said that I should turn my baking into a business, but I never wanted to sell my cakes. In my view, these have been made with love, and you can't buy or sell love."

Eventually, Keren got in touch with a foundation that takes care of children with special needs, and she offered to make each child a special cake for their birthday—a dream cake.

"When I'd visit the foundation, I'd ask every child what their dream cake was. Chocolate? Strawberry? Vanilla? Did they want a cake in the shape of a fairy or a football? In what color? What size? Then I would go and make them precisely the cake they described. And so each child got to fulfill a fantasy and be unique and special. The kids really loved it, and I feel that I was able to find, at last, what to do with my passion."

53

Activate Your Goodness

As you can see, doing good can be so much more than just a hobby or a once a year activity. The more you practice it on a daily basis, the more it will become a way of life. I know this happens because I hear thousands of stories like this from people around the world.

Goodness transforms you on the inside, and as your goodness ripples out to everyone you come in contact with, you'll enjoy a more harmonious life. Next we take this principle—think good, speak good, and do good—and expand it yet again, showing you how to make your goodness reach out to your community and country.

◊   ◊   ◊

CHAPTER FIVE

Doing Good for Your Community and Country

One of the great lessons in my life has been about community and country, and I learned it from my upbringing. As a citizen of both the United States and Israel, very often I felt that I didn't belong in either place. But notwithstanding this, I grew up with the moral values that wherever you live and work, it's important to give back to your community and understand that you are a vital part of it. Everyone can do something, big or small. It's up to the individual to do what they can. This was instilled in me at a very young age, and I've never forgotten it.

Whatever the size of your particular community—it doesn't matter. You might be part of a tribe, a clan, or a tiny village; you might be from a small town or a big city or a remote island surrounded by the vast sea. Whatever the size and shape of the community that you call home, it is your personal responsibility to support the place you live and work.

That is why within all our businesses, Arison Investments is committed to bring about added value to people and society, striving to make a real difference in all the countries where we have operations or investments around the world. We look at all projects from a social, economic, and environmental perspective, following values-based practices in all that we do.

We're just as focused within our philanthropic activities that we make a real difference within our communities and country. Decades ago, I set up the family foundation for my father in Miami to facilitate giving, and when I moved, I created a similar organization called the Ted Arison Family Foundation (TAFF) headquartered in Israel. Listening to the needs of the community, it is through TAFF that we invest in worthwhile social projects in Israel in the fields of education, health, disabilities, culture, arts, and sports. In addition, TAFF is deeply committed to supporting our youth and assisting populations in distress.

Through TAFF, we also created several vision ventures, such as Matan (Your Way to Give), which is modeled on the United Way. In establishing Matan, we became a catalyst for corporate giving, encouraging businesses and employees to donate in order to meet the needs of their communities, thereby creating a culture of giving that had not been present in Israel before then.

Another venture is the Essence of Life, which I previously mentioned. It came from my vision that in order to reach world peace, each one of us needs to reach peace within our own self first. The Essence of Life organization spreads seeds of awareness and gives tools for attaining inner peace through a broad and holistic approach.

The Seeds of Good Deeds

Through the family foundation, we adopted a wonderful organization named Ruach Tova (Good Spirit), which connects individuals who want to volunteer with organizations in need of volunteers. Citizens in Israel are encouraged to volunteer, and so are visitors from other countries who may want to participate in community work while visiting in Israel.

It has been through Ruach Tova that Good Deeds Day in Israel has been managed and has grown in popularity to become International Good Deeds Day. Through the success of Good Deeds Day, I saw the opportunity to create "Goodnet," an innovative online hub, which I'll talk more about later in this book.

I see many good deeds being done in Israel, and when I travel, I know that there are many good people in this world who really care. For example, on a recent trip to New York City, I saw signs asking for volunteers to help clean up litter in Central Park. Doing this kind of thing doesn't take money; it just takes your willingness to do good.

There are many reasons for doing good, but sometimes people just shrug their shoulders and say, "What difference could I make? I'm just one person." But that isn't so—anyone can make a difference.

Perhaps you've heard the well-known story about the starfish that I believe was inspired by the writings of Loren Eiseley. It seems that once upon a time, there was an older man who was walking along the shore one morning when he saw a young man up ahead. As he caught up to him, he could see the young man reaching down, over and over again, picking up starfish one at a time and gently throwing them into the ocean.

He asked the young man, "Why are you doing that?" The young man explained that the sun was coming up and the tide was going out. If he didn't

Activate Your Goodness

throw them back, they would die. The older man was quick to point out, "But don't you realize that there are miles of this beach and thousands of starfish all along it. You can't possibly make a difference!" The younger man listened politely, then bent down to pick up another starfish and threw it into the sea, saying, "Well, it made a difference for that one!"

You too can make a difference. There are so many ways to give to your community and your city; I encourage you to choose something that you like to do. See what your community needs and make it happen. You can do this by volunteering your time or giving a donation. Even if you aren't interested in becoming a volunteer, or you lack the extra money to give to a cause, there are many ways you can do good on your own, such as picking up a piece of litter you see, holding the door for the person behind you, or giving up your seat to someone on the bus.

Touching the Lives of Others

When I think about doing good for communities and countries, I'm fascinated each year by the creativity of people to come up with so many ways to do good. Many initiatives in our own country and other places around the world have crossed cultural boundaries, which is so exciting to me.

One moving experience that I'll never forget was seeing the faces of a group of elderly Holocaust survivors when they heard the first notes being played in a special concert for them. Such a fusion of cultures came together: a choir from the occupied territories, joined by their band and conductor, had crossed the border and arrived in Israel to perform for the Holocaust survivors. The extent of emotion and positivity that swept through the audience was incredible. The international media who were in attendance couldn't contain their feelings either; everyone was so deeply touched by the outpouring of love and goodness in the air.

Activate Your Goodness

In another community, Arab and Jewish children worked together to spruce up their environments. Students from the two schools collaborated to create a joint, open artwork, by painting the long wall that separated their adjoining neighborhoods. They decorated the wall with slogans for peace that were in both Hebrew and Arabic. Hearts were brought closer together, friendships were formed, and a notion was instilled on that day that no wall can separate people who are united in doing good.

Yet another vivid memory I have is of the look in one woman's eyes, as she held my hand when we walked along to see a Good Deeds Day project in Jerusalem. "No one has ever paid any attention to us, no one ever approaches here," she told me earnestly. "It's the first time that anyone has cared about us. Look what's happening today!" she exclaimed and pointed to a large group of people cleaning and renovating the run-down neighborhood. "We're all working together—neighbors, soldiers, and volunteers from youth organizations. It's not the paint or tools they brought that allowed for all this to happen—it's their captivating spirit of good."

Of course, it's not just on this one day, and it's not just in one country; we know that personal and collective acts of good happen all the time all around the world. Every day in our communities, as we go about our daily lives, we see people performing acts of kindness. Why is it then, when we look at the news, we don't really see any of this compassion or goodness being reflected?

In fact, too often it's just the opposite . . . and that's where our story goes next: exploring the many ways our world is reflected back to us, and what we can do to bring out goodness.

◊   ◊   ◊

CHAPTER SIX

Reflections of Doing Good

When we turn on any news report or open a newspaper, more often than not we are bombarded by nothing but bad news—reports of war, chaos, violence, disasters, and so many other kinds of heartbreaking situations. I believe that many of us are deeply impacted on a personal level by what we see reflected back to us by the media; it's easy enough to see how people can become afraid and depressed.

I always thought the news was supposed to show us our true lives and our society. But does it really? The news shows us so many bad things, but are all the things in our world bad? No, of course not. Every

Activate Your Goodness

day we meet people who are helpful and kind—those who pitch in to help when we are in need; we interact with professionals like doctors and firefighters who are there to help people and society every single day. Our world is definitely not as dismal and hopeless as the media would have us believe.

One challenge is that many men and women who work in the media tend to lean toward negative headlines and sensational stories when they report on events that are happening in our world. I agree that the content in our newspapers and on our airwaves could be better, but we can't simply blame journalists, news programmers, or the stations; they're just showing what they believe will get the best ratings or sales. We are the ones who read, watch, and listen to the news; and as parents, we may continue to let our children watch certain shows even if we question its values.

What it really comes down to is a matter of mutual responsibility: the media and all of us together are responsible for improving the situation and raising the quality of what is written in the newspaper, heard on the radio, or seen on TV or online. Instead of blaming and complaining, it's up to us to request a higher standard of content and programming if we don't want to continue to be fearful, sad, and depressed.

Personally, I made a conscious choice years ago to stop reading newspapers and watching the news because it's crippling for me. I felt like it was bringing me down and depleting my energy. When I used to read and watch the news every day, with all its drama and chaos, I felt unable to create the world that I would rather live in.

Of course, as I am a businesswoman, I do get a daily report of what's going on but in a factual way. So I know what the markets are doing and what is happening in the world, but it's just the highlights and the facts, without all the sensationalism.

Seeking Media That Is More Uplifting

Once I was able to think clearly, I wondered how I could constructively begin to help create

Activate Your Goodness

a better world when it comes to media coverage. What I wanted to do is try to show the people in the media how they can reflect and create a better world through reporting and developing programs for newspapers, TV, radio, and the Internet that are more positive and uplifting than what we are used to seeing.

Because I understand that the media is a strong force for creating change, and I wanted to find a way to help people in the media to report more positively or at least in a more balanced way, I established the Shari Arison Center for Communication Awareness at the Interdisciplinary Center (IDC) in Hertzliya.

Within their program, the students learn all the basics about media training for print, radio, TV, and the Internet; but we at the Center wanted to give the students something extra to help them in their careers and their lives. We give them the awareness and the tools they'll need to create programming that better reflects the positive world we would all like to see.

The Center for Communication Awareness also reaches out to working journalists and media writers in the field to promote the concept that the media has the power to create its own future. We ask both the students and the people in the media what they want our collective future to look like and how can they help create it. The students also decided to engage professionals working in the field to become judges or mentors for their student projects, thus engaging everyone in the challenge to create more interesting and thought-provoking kinds of reporting and programming.

Each year the students create projects based on a different theme. Some of the students chose to challenge the public through the Internet to also get involved by sending in video clips. One year the theme was about sustainability and called "Eco Clip," in which a number of videos were made highlighting ways to sustain the environment. Engagement with the students and the public was very high because thousands of people got involved in sending in ideas and clips.

Activate Your Goodness

This year, many inspiring projects were produced at the Center under the theme of "Oneness" and were aimed at showing in creative ways how we are all connected. It was wonderful to watch the student presentations, and one of my favorites was called "Gigglers.tv."

The students who created Gigglers.tv set it up as an online video channel that plays hundreds of video clips of people laughing from around the globe. To get it started, the students searched for the funniest videos on the web and edited the most entertaining laughs into ten-second clips. The platform encourages users to upload their own videos of people laughing and share specific laughs with friends.

The intention of Gigglers.tv was to show how laughter is a universal language, which crosses all borders, and to reinforce the proven fact that laughter has therapeutic effects on the mind and body. This group's motto is to spread the laughter and turn the world into a happier place.

Another fabulous production from students at the Center focused on a toilet. The video was done in a creative and dramatic way to show that although one person is involved in this simple, private daily act, it actually takes a whole host of people to create all the necessary elements that go into building the bathroom, installing the plumbing, and managing water systems. While it might seem like a personal act, the video showed how many people in the world were actually involved in making the drywall, the tiles, the toilet, and the toilet paper; how many others were involved in manufacturing and installing the pipes and the plumbing; and how yet others were involved in the sewer systems and water-treatment plants.

No one really thinks of all these interconnections that are related to the act of using a toilet, so I found the examination of it that the students created was just fascinating. The short video clearly shows how we are all connected through the smallest of daily activities.

Activate Your Goodness

Finding a Balanced Perspective

Our ultimate goal at the Center is to encourage a shift within the media toward depicting a more balanced look at the world. We'd like everyone to see all news events in a good light, which I know sounds little bit crazy. And I'm not just talking about "good news stories," which are often some kind of heartwarming story that you see during the last two minutes of a regular newscast, so they can say they ended on a positive note. No, I'm talking about looking at all news and the events of our world in a way that helps people understand how solutions can be found. We want to illustrate how we can create the future that we all want to see collectively: a positive future for us all.

It's taken a few years, but now we're seeing that people in the media who have been interacting with us at the Center are starting to let go of their cynicism and get on board with a new style of reporting that is inspiring and uplifting, in a more collective and positive way.

This is not to oversimplify things. I'm not saying we have to look at war in a good light. We all know that isn't going to work. But what if we take the reality of war, what it does to a country and to a people, and use that knowledge to get each of us to think and truly ask ourselves, *Is this what I want to see in my world—all this destruction and violence?* If not, then we have to dig deep inside ourselves, understand our inner conflict and how it's reflected in the world, so we can see what actions we can take individually and collectively to create a better reality.

Sometimes it's not even the conflict itself, but the fear we feel when we hear about conflict that is about to happen—such as telling the viewers, over and over again, that tensions are rising in this or that country, terrorist threats are increasing, or the level of violence is much higher than the year before. We, as a collective population, begin to worry more and more, obsess about stories, and consume ourselves with thoughts of impending violence because that is all we're seeing on the news. I'm not saying to ignore wars and violence; rather, let's see how we can bring these situations around to a more positive discussion with positive solutions.

Ultimately, through our efforts at the Center for Awareness Communication, we're helping more people in the media to realize that they have a choice. We're just asking each of them to consider not doing so much writing "against" things, and consider the power of writing "for" things that are truly important, understanding that we have the collective power to create what we want to see in the world.

Delivering Inspiration in Your Own Way

So many uplifting stories have come to my attention. When we encouraged people to share their personal examples of doing good for the greater good, the following story came in from a businessman named Ron who used the power of doing good to create the change he wanted to see.

Ron drives a bus, and when he pulls it into the parking lot of his hometown's only school, the children surround it with shouts of joy, almost as if it were an ice-cream truck. But this bus has no seats, and no chocolate or vanilla—instead, it holds a sophisticated, sparkling science laboratory.

"This was my school," Ron explains with a wave of his hand. "We didn't have computers or practical science classes, because there was never enough money to set up labs or buy computer equipment."

Ron became interested in computers when he was very young. Since his school couldn't provide tools for learning, he went three times a week to the nearest larger town, taking two buses each way, so he could study computer science and mathematics at a university-run enrichment program.

"My mother raised me alone and worked two jobs, but education was always the most important thing in our home. On birthdays and holidays, I never got a bicycle or new clothes—I was given books," Ron remembers.

Activate Your Goodness

Ron turned out to be a gifted student. By the time he was in his 30s, he had become a very successful and energetic entrepreneur. "To my great happiness, I now have enough time and money to be able to give back to the community where I grew up. I bought this old bus and turned it into a mobile laboratory, and once a month, I take time off from work and bring with me several teachers who are also donating their time and knowledge.

"We come here and spend three days with the children. It's so enjoyable to see them open up to the marvelous possibilities contained in science," he continues with a joyful spark. "I tell every one of them that if they stick with it and invest themselves, I'll be happy to give them a job at my company one day."

In the evenings, after he straightens up the bus at the end of another busy day, he goes to stay with his mother, who still lives in the same house where he grew up. "She is the program's biggest supporter, but that could be because it gives her a chance to spoil me for three days in a row every month," he smiles. And he adds with pride, "I dedicated the lab to her. Written on the bus are the words *The Sarah Cohen Mobile Laboratory.* I never could have gotten to where I am today without my mother's support."

Ron grew up in a modest home but made the most of every opportunity. He did not protest in the streets about the lack of school funding for the sciences, or complain bitterly to the government that they should "do something" about the situation. Instead Ron asked himself, *What can I do personally to improve the learning environment for students in a small town? How can I inspire them toward science as a career choice?* He combined his resources and took time out of his own life to deliver inspiration in a fun and exciting way to children who otherwise might not have the chance for a hands-on laboratory experience.

Positive stories like Ron's happen in communities everywhere, as people do what they can to make the world a better place in some specific way. But the media doesn't always present us with the

Activate Your Goodness

full picture of our incredible world. Next time, when your community or country is facing a serious situation, try to shift your own thinking from one of fear and protest to a creative solution that might be outside the box.

When you think good, speak good, and do good, your goodness will ripple out in the way Ron's did and effect a change that will probably be even more awe-inspiring than you can imagine. It only takes a small act to change the world.

◊   ◊   ◊

CHAPTER SEVEN

Doing Good
for Humanity

Sometimes it feels like we're all at war with each other, but you know what? If the Earth were suddenly invaded by another planet, then I expect we'd pretty quickly figure out that we as a human race are united. The geographic boundaries, power struggles between nations, tension between the races . . . all would pale in comparison to the common foe, and we would face it as one.

I sincerely hope we don't need such a catastrophic situation to make everyone realize that we're in this world together. It's true. I've long believed we're all connected—every soul alive on

Activate Your Goodness

this Earth at this time is connected to each other. We are all one. I'm not alone in this belief; many philosophers, humanitarians, and leaders throughout the ages believe it, too.

I hope my words are helping you feel it as well—to feel this connection to all of humanity. Throughout this book, I've been describing in many ways how we're connected, and how goodness ripples out from each of us when we activate our goodness. But still, of course, there is also darkness in the world. This becomes something that is hard to reconcile and to know what to do with—but here's how I see it.

I believe that there is a tipping point with all this energy in the world, and I do realize that it can go either way. There is positive and negative energy, and people will say that this is a given: there will always be a struggle between good and bad, and it will never tip completely in one direction. Yet I believe we can move the tipping point in the direction we want it to go. We can move it more quickly toward good if we continue to create a critical mass of people doing good, choosing good, and thinking good. Once that happens, we will suddenly see a different world.

The challenge is that we really have to try hard to keep good thoughts and actions as our first priority because goodness by its very nature is more subtle, soft, and quiet, compared to badness, which is a much more in-your-face kind of thing, with lots of drama and power.

Getting This Message to the Masses

To ensure a future that is good for us, that is good for all humanity, we need a critical mass of people doing good. Even after the first Good Deeds Day, I could tell that we were headed in the right direction. I could see the success build each year with more and more people coming out to do good.

To build on these strengths and harness the power of the Internet, we at Arison decided to develop and launch the **Goodnet.org** website

Activate Your Goodness

(Goodnet for short). Goodnet was designed to be a Gateway to Doing Good—the first and only portal of its kind. Goodnet inspires and empowers users to independently take positive action, anytime, anywhere, and in any field of interest closest to their hearts. The site connects all people and organizations who are doing good in order to create a critical mass that much quicker.

In our planning and development of Goodnet, our team recognized two main facts. The first was that there are many people worldwide who share a common desire to do good. And second: that there are a tremendous number of organizations and initiatives who do good work year-round, and they are seeking members and participants. There seemed to be an interest in sharing, discussing, and exchanging ideas about doing good; so we wanted to provide a channel for this kind of conversation.

The site places value on collaboration instead of competition—so within the "Good Directory," there's room for all kinds of organizations, social-enterprise websites, and apps in a variety of categories: volunteering and fundraising, nutrition, human rights, and so much more. There is room for everyone to collaborate.

We now have more than 500 organizations featured in the Good Directory, and there's a loud and clear sentiment of eagerness to join forces and generate more good-doing and engage more good-doers. The bottom line is that doing good is easy, and doing good together can create positive change.

In no time at all, organizations and individuals logged on to activate their goodness. Now it's your turn! Before turning the next page, go to **www.goodnet.org**, and activate your goodness. It's easy, quick, and powerful—in doing so, with a simple click, you're adding your voice and efforts to the cause of good in this world. You're already connected to everyone else just through your birth into the human race. You are already doing acts of goodness!

Through joining Goodnet, you'll show that you are connected and committed to a world filled

Activate Your Goodness

with universal good. You'll find enlightening stories and videos of all kinds of "good" things on this site. The critical mass is growing minute by minute—perhaps your goodness will be the catalyst and cause the tipping point! Who knows?

On Goodnet, you will find a stream of content that is updated daily. These are grab-and-go stories about organizations, products, websites, and apps that are all about doing good in three circles: *me, people,* and *planet.* So whenever you want to find organizations that align with your own beliefs and values, consider the Good Directory. If you're looking for easy and doable activities, we provide a bi-weekly newsletter called *Activate Your Goodness.*

We also offer "Good TV," which is a series of uplifting videos for inspiration and good vibes. The video entries are gathered from the Web and are often suggested by our readers (individuals and organizations). Goodnet helps promote "Good Conversation" so that our visitors can engage in conversation on topics related to doing good: on the website and within social-media channels.

Creating Our Collective Future

As a collective, I believe that we can find ways to work together to solve the problems that we're facing as a human race. When we each take personal responsibility, we can create the collective future that we all want. Sites like Goodnet and books like this one help show you just how similar we all are to each other in this world.

In the big scheme of things, we all want to be happy and at peace; we all want to feel fulfilled in our daily lives. We all want health, we all want to prosper, and we all want a safe environment for our children and for ourselves. Deep down, we all want these same things. They are universal human desires regardless of your background or where you live.

Our need to feel fulfilled and connected is powerful. I've seen and heard many stories of people who reached out to others through good deeds and ended up feeling a deep sense of fulfillment and connection. One of these people is Elinor, who

Activate Your Goodness

shared her personal example of doing good; hers was one of the many incredible stories we at Arison heard about through Good Deeds Day.

Elinor reached out of her own comfort zone to connect with other people through sharing a universal gift—the gift of music. In doing so, she not only felt the ripple of good go out from herself, which gave her a new sense of connection to people within her community, but she also felt the ripple of goodness come back to her in the form of greater self-esteem, confidence, and happiness.

Her story begins with her describing what it's like to be painfully shy. "I had a terrible fear of audiences," Elinor says earnestly. "Even at my own wedding, I was full of anxiety. I didn't want to come out and stand in front of the guests who had come to celebrate the joyous day with me—and these were my close friends and relatives. I always yearned to sing, but since you can't go out onstage wearing a mask, I knew this would be impossible, too."

However, the opportunity to burst free came by chance at a costume party she attended.

"They had a karaoke machine there, and I was standing in the corner, shy to the point of being terrified, yet I was burning with the desire to sing. Suddenly I realized that no one would recognize me because I was actually wearing a mask!" Able to hide behind her costume, Elinor got up to sing and finished to wild cheers. "But I knew it was a onetime thing—after all, I couldn't go around all the time in a mask like the Phantom of the Opera."

When she told a friend about what had happened, how much she would love to be able to sing again in public, her friend said, "I know just where you can sing." She told Elinor about a club for blind people, and the idea to perform for them appealed to her. She carefully chose the songs and practiced for days, and a week later, she joined her friend when she went to the club.

Elinor sighs as the memory washes over her, when she thinks of how far she has come since that particular day. "I've appeared before many people since then, but that was and always will be the most exciting performance of my life. The love I felt coming back from the audience was amazing, and it liberated me from the shyness and fear I had always felt."

After that performance, Elinor started to appear regularly at that club and in many others. Through doing good, she now radiates a sense of confident ease, getting up often to sing for the members of a local seniors' club and filling her own life with happiness and joy. Her rich voice fills the auditorium, and the words of the old love songs she sings flow from her so tenderly that tears spring to the eyes of her listeners. "Maybe some of them can't see me with their eyes, but they look at me with their hearts, and that's all I ever needed."

Focusing on the Collective Good

Our connectedness with the human race is always there, but sometimes it takes a conscious act for us to feel it and realize its tremendous power. When we focus our energies on improving our world through goodness, we enjoy many benefits.

Sometimes when I think about humanity, I see it as very similar to the human body. The body has all of these different organs and systems and parts: each one of them is individual but has its own critical role in supporting human life and overall health. And it's like this in our world when we think of humanity: we have many diverse peoples, who speak different languages, enjoy different cultures, and live in different countries. All parts of humanity have different roles that each person, community, and country play; but in the end, we're all just one human race, just as our body is one body.

But what happens when one part of the body attacks another part of the body? You get cancer or a catastrophic illness. This is what violence within humanity is causing—a cancer. Violence or fighting of any kind causes the whole of humanity to be sick, and this can become like a life-threatening disease if we don't resolve the violence we experience.

Activate Your Goodness

When we focus instead on the collective good rather than destruction or confrontation, we bring healing energy to the human race. More and more we're seeing this truth play out in our lives; and we're seeing this theme covered in books, movies, and on the Web. I just saw a movie on YouTube called *I AM* and in it, there were powerful images of how we're all connected and how small acts can truly change things; it illustrates the ripple effect in motion in our world.

Everywhere you look today, you will see that the masses are starting to speak out. This is a good thing, but be aware that it only really works for goodness if you're speaking out with a message and actions that produce a positive change. I worry that too many are speaking out through protest, anger, and violence; they might think they are trying to change the world for the best, but any kind of protest against anything, even if it is for a good cause, is still a fight.

Therefore, I encourage you to go out and talk about what you are "for" instead of what you are "against." What positive solutions can you come up with to create the world you would rather have? Remember, we are all one.

I recognize that this is a shift, and it can be hard to do, but it's worth it. For years within my companies and management teams, I'd always hear people say why something couldn't be done. And I'd challenge them to think about it and gain a fresh perspective, and then come back and tell me how it could be achieved. Eventually, the shift happened and very creative solutions and positive ideas started becoming the norm; and that's when true organizational transformation really took off.

So the challenge for you is to put this concept to work in your life. We all must take personal responsibility for coming up with new ideas and solutions to the issues we face today. Collective, positive solutions will move us toward a collective, positive future. This is the gift we give to ourselves and to our world when we choose goodness and take action toward it. Our goodness

Activate Your Goodness

ripples out from humanity to our planet and the
environment, which are the two ripples we will
explore next.

◇   ◇   ◇

CHAPTER EIGHT

Doing Good
for the Planet

When I first thought about sustainability within my companies, more than a dozen years ago, I tried to develop a new vision for Shikun & Binui (our global construction, real-estate, and infrastructure company). I wanted to create "Apartments of Light," so people could live in places with large windows that would allow an abundance of natural light. I wanted these apartments to convey a good feeling, be surrounded by greenery, and be built with consideration for the environment and in harmony with nature.

But back then, my vision was ahead of its time. The leaders within the company couldn't understand why I was going on and on about sustainable construction, and they were quite determined it would never really work. But I remained steadfast in my own determination, and gradually a few of my managers began to come on board with this concept, agreeing to take a serious look at how it might work.

Then those of us who wanted it to happen got a boost in our efforts when Al Gore's film, *An Inconvenient Truth*, was released. Its powerful environmental message helped the others in the company appreciate that this vision had merit. Suddenly, people woke up and understood it was time to act. It was a great day when the management team and the board of directors agreed we would set a new vision of becoming leaders in the emerging field of sustainable development within the real-estate and infrastructure industry.

Of course, this isn't the kind of vision that can be completely realized overnight, and there will always be those who criticize and only see what is not perfect. Such processes take time, a lot of time, but the important thing is that we have successfully embarked on our journey, and it's working. Shikun & Binui builds so much more than just apartments—for decades, the company has been building roads, highways, bridges, and neighborhoods. Today, they are leaders in all kinds of infrastructure projects using 100 percent sustainable practices. These practices not only protect the environment from harm, but they also focus on doing good for the planet and for people in many creative and innovative ways.

Over the years, Arison Investments has become a business entity that invests in and impacts all vital facets of life—finance, real estate, infrastructure, water, and energy—and we're developing management strategies that take a comprehensive, long-term view of all the aspects: economic, social, and environmental. Through our values-based businesses, we are pursuing this as a long-term vision with passion. We are providing a response to universal human needs, from which we derive business potential as well as adding value for the human race.

Activate Your Goodness

Making Personal Choices for Our Planet

In our lives, it very often takes a dramatic event to happen for us to take action, and this is especially true when we think about environmental awareness. I've experienced several dramatic events myself that have opened my eyes to the reality of our interconnectedness and has led me to be so passionate about the need for all our actions—at home and at work—to be sustainable.

I believe that everyone in the world deserves to breathe clean air, but this conviction grew even stronger in my heart and mind after I visited certain countries in the Far East. I already knew we needed to care for the air in our world and keep it clean, but when I saw people having to walk around with masks on because of the pollution, I understood even more fully what it means to live in a place where it's almost impossible to breathe.

This was years ago, when there was a lower level of environmental awareness as compared to today, and I think most of the world took too much for granted. I know I did. We thought we would always have fresh air, clean water, and enough healthy food to sustain us.

I thought for a long time that I would work in the field of clean air, but then I realized that I couldn't do everything. Through intuition and a calling from my soul, I chose to go into the field of water, understanding that water is life. I also saw clearly that the world focuses too much on scarcity, when it would be much better to see our future as abundant. Therefore, I created a water efficiency company called Miya with the mandate to sustain the water we already have. Miya develops practical technologies for countries and communities around the world to efficiently manage water systems, so our precious water supply isn't wasted.

I was also deeply affected by a visit to Africa that led me to adopt a strict vegetarian lifestyle. It was there that I came to truly understand nature and respect it. I saw that every creature is a creature of God. The vibrancy of colors, the sunrises, the sunsets, the freedom, the animals—all of this opened my soul.

But the most dramatic event happened one day when I went out to feed the giraffes at a ranch in Kenya. At a restaurant that evening, they served us a delicacy: giraffe. From that moment on, I have not touched any meat.

Several years later, I learned about the Jain sect in India. In one of their ceremonies, I saw how they walk with a broom and sweep the earth in front of them in order to avoid harming any living creatures, not even killing an ant by mistake. It touched my heart so deeply, and it was another powerful reminder to me that we are all God's creatures, great and small.

These experiences shaped my attitude toward nature, and my emerging beliefs were made even more real after I read a book entitled *Mutant Message Down Under* by Marlo Morgan, which tells of an American woman's experiences with a tribe of Aboriginal Australians.

These are the reasons why I have decided to no longer use anything that causes suffering to an animal. I can't understand how so many people can sit on sofas or wear handbags and shoes that are made of leather, and they don't realize how many animals had to die for that. I'm not saying that everyone has to make sacrifices and give things up; that's not realistic. I'm not perfect, and neither is anyone else, but we can all do our part, whatever feels right for us.

The Healing Touch

You don't have to look far in our world to see how powerfully we are connected to nature and animals. One of my strongest memories from Good Deeds Day illustrates this; it was at a kindergarten for children with special needs. We gathered there to help bring smiles to the young children who were suffering with quite severe disabilities, and we were aided by small animals from a petting zoo.

Activate Your Goodness

Rabbits were softly caressed by the little hands, hamsters were held and tickled, turtles waddled along. I was profoundly moved as I was invited to play alongside these children and help them pet the friendly animals. I was on our Good Deeds Day tour, and I was just about to move along with the tour and the media to the next site when the kindergarten teacher approached me excitedly. She told me that a certain child there suffered from a severe case of sensual over-sensitivity, but he bravely overcame his problem and gently touched the animals that were brought over to him. She said his smile will remain in her heart forever.

I have come to fully accept the universal truth that we are all connected, we are all one. And although this certainly applies to us as a human race, we humans are connected to *all* elements of our world: earth, animals, nature, air, and water.

When we accept this view of ourselves and our connection to our world, we can then begin to understand the old world and the reasons for its collapse. We're all affected by what happens in our world—good or bad. For example, I believe that the natural disasters we've been seeing rise up of late, including their increased numbers and the intense devastation they are causing—namely earthquakes, tsunamis, forest fires, droughts, and floods—are signs of a wound that the Earth is cleansing itself of. Our planet has a need to cleanse itself from years of built-up negative energy, the same way we cleanse ourselves through introspection and doing good.

It's interesting to consider that as long as the dramatic changes in our world just involved nature, people could still choose not to see the truth or face the need for change. But now we see that the global financial crisis has led many people to internalize the fact that the old world no longer works. World economies and government structures that were based on old models of scarcity, fear, and power struggles are crumbling and making way for the new world.

I believe that this is why so many people are affected in such a profound way just by hearing about financial crises and violence in our world; we are all connected. You may feel these things on an emotional level or sometimes physically, even though you might not have been directly hurt by the downturns or by the wars in other countries.

Reaching a Deeper Connection

I believe the reason that all this is being felt so deeply now is because there is a greater level of general awareness of our connectedness through the Internet. It's no longer possible to conceal the collapse and the inner war that rages below the surface individually or collectively. The world has become transparent, and we can see and feel how fragile and chaotic things have become around us.

It comes back to where we started. When we experience chaos inside ourselves, we see chaos reflected in our world. As we resolve our internal chaos and cleanse ourselves (which we know we can do by doing good), the end result will be a better world.

Now we can see that the push toward environmental sustainability is about so much more than just going green. Spirituality is rising, and we accept that the Earth itself is a living, breathing entity—the trees, the animals, our relationships . . . everything has energy. Within our connectedness, we as humans are diminished when any part of nature is harmed, and I think it's time for all of us to reflect more deeply on this. When you harm anything else that is living, you actually harm yourself because we are all one.

I realize that these concepts are complex, and there is so much that can be done. It might seem somewhat overwhelming, and you might not know where to start. So my advice is—start somewhere. Act in as bold a way as you can in your protection of nature, our environment, and our planet. As an individual, you can start by cleaning up your own yard or neighborhood. You can learn about sustainability, and do something, no matter how small. Every little act counts because the little acts together become one big action.

Activate Your Goodness

If you are a teacher or professor, you can challenge your students to incorporate sustainable concepts or actions within their schoolwork or projects, regardless of how young they might be. If you run a company, you can inspire teams of employees to identify sustainable initiatives within your operations, and you can supply resources so that the good ideas can be implemented. As a worker anywhere in your organization, you can encourage your fellow employees and the management team to take positive steps.

As a scientist or researcher, you may be on the cusp of discovering new environmental realities that we will hear about and be able to act upon. If you're in a leadership role, or you are an actor or a gifted public speaker, you can inspire others through your actions and your words. As a journalist, you can report on good news and positive actions being taken by citizens so others can learn from those examples. Anyone, anywhere can do their part.

As you do good for the planet and the environment in any way you can, be it taking on a complex challenge or a simple daily act, you add to the collective will; and it's my belief that when enough people take action, we'll reach a tipping point. Once our collective actions tip the scale toward environmental protection and sustainability, these actions and values will become a way of life, transforming ourselves and our world.

Collectively, we have the power to bring out the most beautiful and peaceful essence in ourselves and in our world that we have ever seen. I can't wait, and neither can the planet! Think good, speak good, and do good; the time for action is now.

❖   ❖   ❖

CHAPTER NINE

How Doing Good Transforms Your Life

So if it's my wish to motivate you to act, what else can I say? Have I exhausted all my points in this case? No, not by a long shot. This book would never be finished if it was necessary for me to come to a conclusion, because once the ripples of goodness start flowing, they are so powerful that they have no beginning and no end. They cannot be stopped!

I firmly believe that this theory of mine—that doing good will change the world—will win over any remaining doubters, and eventually, we'll be able to bring everyone aboard this train. Please

Activate Your Goodness

consider this as your ticket to journey with us, to join us in doing good each day. Membership to our group is simple: There are no membership fees or dues to pay. Just begin with any act of goodness, and you are a member in good standing.

Perhaps you might still need a bit of persuasion, though, or you know of other people around you who might not yet be willing to join in. If so, let's take a moment to consider four personal benefits that you'll enjoy as you make the conscious choice to think good, speak good, and do good.

First, doing good builds self-esteem and self-confidence. Second, doing good makes you a leader and an inspiration to others. Third, doing good brings out your very best attributes. And fourth, doing good brings you more happiness and joy to your life.

Expanding Your Self-Esteem

Let's explore the first point, how doing good builds your self-esteem and self-confidence. It works on all levels. On a physical level, think about the times when you're not feeling good about your body. You may then dress in older clothes, and you feel like no matter what you're wearing, it doesn't look good on you. You just generally feel awful.

Whereas when you do good things to take care of yourself, such as taking time to dress nicely each day, you feel better. When you put on makeup, or for a man you take time to shave and perhaps put on aftershave, it really makes such a difference. I think generally all people feel better when they take care of themselves.

You can then look in the mirror and say, "Wow, I look good today!" I know I've been there; at times in my life it made a huge difference when I made a conscious choice to take better care of myself. For me, that means starting out each day by going out for a run or a walk and taking time to meditate— that way I feel much more confident about having a bright day.

On an emotional level, when you're feeling sad and depressed, you may also find yourself

Activate Your Goodness

complaining about all the things that aren't going well in your life, focusing only on thoughts like, *He hurt my feelings* or *She made me angry.* In this case, you're just not going to feel good about yourself because you're not in that state of mind. But if you change your mind-set and try not to dwell so much on those things, and try to think more positively about the day and what it holds, you will quite likely find that life flows so much better. It's a natural outcome of how you're thinking and feeling, and if your actions are ones that you can be proud of, then you will have more confidence and enjoy greater self-esteem.

I heard about a story of a woman who had moved into a shelter because she had been abused by a male partner. She was very scared to leave the shelter, since she might be recognized and didn't have any extra money to buy makeup or get her hair done. Fortunately for her, a man who owned a salon heard about women like her from a case-worker at the shelter, and he offered to help. He agreed to stay open certain times at night so that these women could come in privately. He would provide his services for free and give them a new look and a bit of pampering at the salon. He asked one of his friends who was a makeup artist to help him, too.

It worked out amazingly well. One woman was so grateful because by taking care of herself better, she now has more self-esteem and self-confidence. "For years the only color I had on my face was the bluish-purple of my bruises. Today, thanks to this wonderful place, I know how to put on makeup, I take good care of myself, and I feel good in my femininity."

Bringing Out Your Inner Leader

Now, let's consider the second point. I believe that doing good makes you a leader and an inspiration to others. Personally, I've always been inspired by people who have made a difference in the world, such as Martin Luther King, Jr.; Gandhi; or Mother Teresa. I've always looked up to them. And I not

Activate Your Goodness

only admire high-profile people, but also anyone who is doing extraordinary things in this world. Whether they're using their professional training or their natural gifts, they're an inspiration to me.

I once saw on an international show a story about a doctor who went to a small village in South America and helped citizens there who had lost a limb or had been born without one. He was able to fit them with an artificial one, and he made such an incredible difference to those people. This doctor gave these people a much better quality of life, and they were so grateful. He used his gifts for this greater good, and even though very few could pay for his service, it didn't matter to him. I find this very uplifting.

There was another fascinating story about a man who wanted to help drug addicts who were homeless. He knew which section of town they stayed in, so he made a point to take his daily run each day through those run-down neighborhoods. Each day he would jog by them, and slowly over time, some of these homeless people began running with him. And then eventually, several of them stopped doing drugs because they started to feel better about their bodies, better about their lives.

I was moved by this story because the man took action though doing good and provided a very quiet, profound inspiration to those individuals. He actually showed them a simple way they could start to feel better. The goodness in his act rippled out over time and made a huge difference. You can do this, too. You can become a leader just through the act of doing good. Others will see you and be inspired.

Even someone quietly sitting on the grass in the park or at the beach meditating, they can serve as an inspiration to someone else. Very often, where one person does this, you'll see others follow their lead. One person joins the first one, then another person joins them, and so on; and you now have a group of people meditating for the benefit of the world, bringing good energy forward. All of a sudden, you have a "leader" just from someone who was sitting quietly.

Activate Your Goodness

In my own community, I was privileged and touched to meet two inspiring leaders, whom I met through a Good Deeds Day interview that they conducted with me. The interview was shown on one of Israel's top news portals, and the two young people were members of Shalva, the Association for Physically and Mentally Challenged Children in Israel. Efrat has Down syndrome and Matanel has special needs, yet they both wanted to find out how they could help get involved on Good Deeds Day.

The interview went very well, and I'm sure that many viewers were moved by the enthusiasm they saw. I was also thrilled to hear that Efrat and Matanel found a great way to get involved on Good Deeds Day. They volunteered to spend time visiting with the elderly and with some children of foreign workers, making a point to make them happy. Even though these two young people have their own challenges, they didn't stop to worry about themselves. They focused instead on giving their time to help others, and they are leaders who are an inspiration to me and many others. Efrat and Matanel went on to create a wonderful film called *Special Interview* where they documented their unique journey trying to realize their dream to interview U.S. President Barack Obama.

Connecting to the Best in Yourself

So now, we'll move on to the third point: how doing good brings out your very best attributes. Doing good reveals all kinds of good qualities, such as kindness, respect, love, compassion, acceptance, patience, and tolerance. When you're doing good for yourself, you become more kind and caring to yourself, and then you have more love to give to others.

Here is an example from my own life. I was in a close personal relationship that opened my heart. Although there were many growing pains, the experience taught me valuable lessons, including patience and acceptance. Through staying focused on doing good for myself and for the other person, I was finally able to learn how to accept people for who they are.

I know now what it is that I want and the importance of being true to myself. I also learned how strong I am inside, and how to trust myself. That was one of the most important lessons for me, learning to let go and be able to trust in the process, trust in God, and trust in the universe. I believe the experience truly brought out attributes hidden deep inside me, and I'm so grateful. All of this happened because I was focused on doing good.

You never know what qualities in yourself you will uncover through doing good. I heard about a scheduler for a taxi company who was always nervous about hospitals. But when one of his drivers was hospitalized for heart surgery, he went in to see him almost every day. The experience opened his eyes to how difficult it is for the patients' families who have to spend so much time waiting around and supporting their loved ones. He could see it wasn't easy for them to have meals, and it was expensive because they weren't at home. If they needed things, it was a challenge to get them; and on top of that, it was very hard at times to understand all the medical words and terms the doctors were using.

As the man explained, "I started to think about how I could help them, and I enlisted all the company's drivers in the effort. One man brought in tea and coffee, and another one brought his daughter, who is a doctor, to explain what was going on. Someone else organized meals for them, and that is how we helped them through the hospitalization period."

When the driver was discharged, the company decided to keep doing this good work; and today, all the drivers are volunteers at hospitals and try to make things easier for the patients' families. They make sure they have something to eat and that there is someone to take care of errands, like paying bills or collecting the children from school—since the drivers are in their taxis and on the roads all day long anyway, it's something they are happy to help with. This experience continues to bring out the very best in each driver as they step up to help in ways they might not have thought they were capable of doing.

Increasing Your Happiness and Joy

For the remainder of this section, I'd like to point out how doing good brings more happiness and joy in your life. Let's start with the thought that goodness is a light energy and light brings joy, happiness, and peace to all it touches. I think it's within our very nature to be happier when we think good, speak good, and do good.

To see the truth in this, you just have to think about how you feel when you *aren't* thinking or doing good. If you're doing things you know aren't nice or that go against nature or that might hurt someone else, you're far more likely to feel guilty, ashamed, and embarrassed than to feel good.

For me, there are many things that bring me joy and happiness. Of course, first and foremost are my children—being with them, watching them grow, and sharing their lives. But there are many more things that make me happy, such as nature, flowers, forests, oceans, music, dancing, a good musical or an uplifting movie, a smile on someone's face, or the joyful sound of laughter.

My passion in this world is to inspire people, whether it's one-on-one or speaking to a group. When I see the twinkle in their eyes and know they're "getting it," I'm so thrilled and happy. When I see the lightbulb coming on for people, and I know I've inspired them to make positive changes for themselves and others, this makes me happier than almost anything else.

For me, this book is another way to get my message out so that people can connect to themselves and resonate their goodness out to all the circles in their lives. Read on to find out how all of our collective efforts are gaining momentum—the critical mass of goodness is coming.

◇　　　◇　　　◇

CHAPTER TEN

International Good Deeds Day

The idea to create Good Deeds Day came to me one morning when I was walking on the sand dunes in Israel, on one of my usual early-morning walks. I thought, *Why not set aside one day each year where everyone is encouraged to do a good deed? All that would be required to participate is a desire to do good.*

The concept for this day was based on my firm belief that each and every one of us can give of ourselves for the benefit of others, according to our own skills and abilities. Everyone can do a good deed and contribute to the community in which they live.

Activate Your Goodness

I thought that doing a good deed could be as simple as just smiling at someone—because smiling at others is a way for you to put your own positive energy out there. Or some people might choose to be part of a larger collective experience on that day—one where people volunteer to help with a community development project.

When a critical mass gathers to do good, so much can be accomplished even in just one day, such as cleaning up a park or beach; painting a community center; or brightening the day for a group of seniors by visiting them to chat, play music, or participate together in games.

When I first spoke to my team about my idea, it made sense to have it organized and managed by Arison's nonprofit organization, Ruach Tova. The first event was held in the spring as a sort of festival of doing good. It gave charitable groups a chance to focus on themselves and promote their cause and good works to the public. It was also a special day for volunteers to shine and celebrate the time they give to causes that are near and dear to their hearts.

As my team and I started to promote the day, we wanted to encourage everyone to participate, either by themselves with a personal act of goodness or to join in with a community project along with their neighbors, fellow workers, or social group. We also welcomed students of all ages, seniors, soldiers . . . anyone at all. Ruach Tova got all kinds of inquiries and matched up many people with specific Good Deeds Day projects that were happening in their communities.

Starting Out in a Simple Way

That year, at our first Good Deeds Day in Israel in 2007, about 7,000 people participated. The team at Ruach Tova and Arison did such an incredible job getting it all organized, and they arranged for me to visit different projects all over the place throughout the day. When we would arrive to

Activate Your Goodness

cheer on the groups, I was emotionally blown away to see the outpouring of love and goodness in the air, along with the smiles of the people who were being helped. The volunteers wore T-shirts that were made up especially for Good Deeds Day, and their enthusiasm was contagious.

In the second year, we began a partnership with the leading Israeli newspaper, getting our message out through their paper and Internet site, and this helped bring out twice as many partici-pants compared to the first year, which was so incredible to see. By year three, it was thrilling that more than 40,000 people from across Israel, and some from the Arab communities, joined in the cause, coming out to help with community projects or do an individual act of good for some-one else.

In the third year, we continued with the news-paper partnership and our usual other promo-tional channels, but we added social media and began getting the word out through Facebook, too. Each year, we heard from more and more organizations and communities that wanted to join in, so our team was busy tracking all the projects and volunteers, and matching up more and more people who contacted us to make sure everyone had something good to do that day.

During the next few years, participation kept growing, and then we started to hear from more and more people outside of Israel who loved the idea and wanted to join in. In 2010, we had about 70,000 people come out to do good deeds, and that number doubled again the next year.

Adding an Online Campaign

As we began planning for 2012, we were really excited because we found an additional promotional sponsor that was a perfect match for us. MTV Europe came on board with us as a strategic partner to help us get the word out worldwide. They helped us develop and implement a full awareness campaign aimed at reaching out to an international audience, particularly to young people.

Activate Your Goodness

MTV International produced a catchy TV and Internet commercial that aired for six weeks before Good Deeds Day in 2012. They created a joint website that they hosted and offered an incentive prize; plus they coordinated all their editorial channels to help us promote the vision. The campaign was a hit, reaching some 24 million views on the TV network. People shared their good deeds on the dedicated website, uploading scores of clips, pictures, and stories.

Not only did this campaign reach 24 countries across Europe, but we also got a tremendous response through social media, which lead to inquires from people in almost 50 different countries. We had managed to take Good Deeds Day international, and in 2012, more than 250,000 people in Israel and thousands more around the world participated in personal and collective acts of goodwill. That year, 163 local authorities in Israel got in the action, including 62 out of 68 Arab municipalities. This is amazing.

There were more than 3,700 projects going on in that one day. There were house-painting projects to assist elderly citizens, groups renovated different schools and day-care centers, teams met to plant community gardens, some chose to play music together for their neighbors, hundreds participated in food drives, and so much more.

It was awe-inspiring to see the wide diversity of projects and ideas that people came up with! Barbers and hair salons cut hair for free for those who couldn't afford it, giving those people a day of pampering that really lifted their spirits. In other cases, free haircuts and new styles were offered to people with long hair; and when possible, the hair that was cut off was donated to organizations that make wigs for people who lose their hair due to cancer.

We heard about a woman in the United Kingdom who did her own act of goodness throughout the year: she would leave her coin in the shopping trolley for the next person—just a small act of personal goodness that would brighten the day for the

Activate Your Goodness

next shopper. In another community, someone got the idea to organize individual street musicians and have them play all together in the main square as an orchestra for everyone to enjoy.

Local charities soon found that Good Deeds Day was a good time to take advantage of the atmosphere to encourage increased donations to their worthy causes and to sign up volunteers who were willing to continue with a commitment to that charity throughout the year, extending their goodwill beyond just the day's events.

Each year as Good Deeds Day grows, we're amazed to see its reach and its impact expanding out around the globe. Whenever anyone does a good deed for the benefit of others or for our planet, the circle of goodness ripples out, and then more and more new people and new communities join in.

In this way, Good Deeds Day serves as an example of what our world can be like all year round, not just on a single day. If we adopt the Good Deeds Day values and take action throughout the year, I'm certain that we'll create a critical mass of people to bring about an essential and lasting change in our world. I'm happy to share just a few of the thousands of actions we've heard about around the world, to inspire you to make your own difference.

Good Deeds Day Spreads Around the World

Imagine the man in India who was devastated to see a big, beautiful old tree fall down near the railway station platform in his community. He could see it had been trimmed too far back by the gardeners, which caused it to fall down. Yet no one at the railway company would admit it, and they refused to help replace it. When they turned away, the man stepped up. "I took the initiative to replant a sapling myself. I did it as a deed to Mother Earth and to all the humans and the birds who took shelter in that old tree."

Activate Your Goodness

We also heard about a creative group in South America who decided to mark Good Deeds Day in Buenos Aries by making a large sign that read: "There is nothing better to do in the world than helping another!" and held it up at a busy intersection. In addition, they handed out candy and notes with suggestions for good deeds to the cars at the traffic light. In this way, they got to see the immediate impact. At first, many stressed-out drivers appeared confused by the gesture, but after receiving the candy and reading the notes, many of them smiled and wished the volunteers a good day, and others even joined in on the activity themselves. From this small act of doing good, a feeling of camaraderie spread throughout the usually hectic intersection.

In the Ukraine, Good Deeds Day was taken a step further and made into a weeklong event in eight different cities, with 10,000 volunteers. One of the more memorable activities was organized by volunteers who arranged a charitable auction of artwork created by orphans and hospitalized children. In addition to sales of the children's paintings, the volunteers gathered secret wishes from these children to create "Trees of Wishes," where each leaf represented one child's dream, and participants of the auction were invited to fulfill a child's dream on the spot. One child made a wish for a new friend, and in response, another child who was there jumped at the opportunity and even offered his stuffed animal to his new pal.

Activities That Transform Lives

In so many cities across the United States, there were an amazing range of group activities and personal acts on Good Deeds Day. For example, a group of employees in New York City joined forces with two social-service groups to volunteer to deliver holiday food packages to homebound citizens on a rainy Sunday morning. One woman had an especially moving experience. After ringing the doorbell at her assigned address, she was greeted by a lovely woman who had put on makeup and

Activate Your Goodness

her favorite dress for the occasion. The two women spent the morning exchanging stories about their families who lived far away, and made a pact to keep meeting every Sunday for brunch.

I also smile when I think about the young woman we heard about from New Jersey, who taught swing-dance lessons to children at an after-school program in an underprivileged neighborhood. For Good Deeds Day, she decided to plan a performance by the kids at a local nursing home in order to provide some entertainment and excitement and brighten their day. She figured since swing music and swing dancing was so popular in the first half of the 20th century, the senior citizens might enjoy the show. The children worked hard on getting their routines ready and even made special T-shirts for the performance. The residents of the nursing home were delighted to have such a youthful and energetic group of visitors, and loved seeing them dance to music from the time when they themselves were growing up.

Then there was a day-care center for the benefit of single mothers in Los Angeles, which was in dire need of a face-lift in order to make the place warmer and more welcoming for the children. A local business in the neighborhood offered to sponsor a fresh layer of paint, and came over with all of their employees on Good Deeds Day to give the dingy walls a new look. A bright and soothing shade of yellow, which was just like sunshine, was chosen by the caregivers of the center, and the group of volunteers happily painted the playroom and even added whimsical stencils of animals. When the children and their mothers came in the next morning, the new decor made them all smile.

In New Hampshire, a young man with a passion for writing wanted to share his short stories. He sought out an audience and found a man who was blind and interested in having company. On Good Deeds Day, the writer made a visit to the man's home and spent the afternoon reading to him. Both benefited from the meeting, as well as making a new friend. The blind man thoroughly enjoyed hearing the stories and offered to lend a listening ear whenever the writer had new material that he wanted feedback on.

In the Raleigh area of North Carolina, more than 100 people participated in Good Deeds Day activities, which included a food collection, distributing lunch at a shelter, donating to families in need, and making holiday baskets for homebound seniors. The baskets were particularly well received, as one man commented, "It was so nice to get a personal package for the holiday, filled with special supplies that I otherwise would have had to go through a lot of trouble to get. But the best part was the note inside, wishing me a happy holiday with a name and phone number, in case I needed help with anything else. That made me feel like there are people who care about others in the community."

Voices Singing Out in Goodness

As you can see, there are endless numbers of good ideas, and there are so many ways to do good.

For every collective event I've mentioned here, there were thousands of other personal acts of goodness that were done by individuals on their own.

It's hard to pick highlights, because I have been blessed to see and hear thousands of wonderful stories of good over the years. But I will share just one more before this chapter ends. I was on my usual Good Deeds Day tour here in Israel, when I heard voices from the trees above me. I looked up to see young people with bags slung over their shoulders climbing up to help a farmer harvest his oranges. Their excited voices rang out in English since they were from America, and when I heard them speaking, I was so excited, I felt like I was coming home. All day I had been surrounded by my team here, the Israeli media, and Hebrew-speaking volunteers; it was an unexpected delight to hear the joyous voices ring out in English, while they were doing their own good deed.

I knew then with certainty that I didn't need to wonder any longer about my roots, about my citizenship—about which country or which world

Activate Your Goodness

I belonged to. It was clear to me on that glorious day that I am American, I am Israeli, I am a citizen of the world as we all are. *We are all one.*

So now each year, in the spring, on International Good Deeds Day, I invite you to do a good deed that will benefit the life of another, make someone else happy, or improve our human condition or natural environment. You know as well as I do that such a good deed will also improve your own life, and will make you happier in your knowledge that you contributed to making our world a better place.

Better yet, why not do good deeds every day? When you think good, speak good, and do good, you'll see that together, in expressing our goodwill and faith in our ability, we're creating a lasting and real change, for us and for future generations.

◊   ◊   ◊

Awakening to a New Choice— a Choice to Do Good

There is so much suffering in the world— poverty, illness, death, destruction. Most of us tend to blame our hardships on something outside of ourselves, something beyond our control. I know I did. Financial situations, breakups, health issues . . . many things we all seem to suffer through at various points in our lives. Of course, everyone experiences setbacks, and some difficulties are out of our control—but in order to grow, does it always have to be intensely painful?

Activate Your Goodness

Where does suffering really occur? I believe it's in our minds, in our hearts, and in our bodies. However, there comes a day—and for each of us the timing is different—when we say, "No more suffering!"

My day came, my lightbulb lit up, when I realized that my suffering was from within. Really, think about it: Where do you "live"? I know that I live in, and view the world through, what I think and what I feel.

That day, I made the conscious decision, the conscious choice that I did not want to suffer anymore. That was when I started living. That's when I acknowledged that I was creating my suffering, and everything outside of me was just a "learning ground." Everything outside of me was there for me to learn and grow. Only after this realization could I make a conscious decision to be happy, healthy, and at peace.

Yes, the road was long, and I'm still traveling it. But every day is a new awakening. Today, I invite you to choose to stop suffering and to become

happy, healthy, and at peace. Find your way—
your own unique way—to achieve this goal. Just
remember: *Do it by doing good.*

◇   ◇   ◇

ACKNOWLEDGMENTS

It would take a whole book to list all the names of the people I would like to thank; please know that I appreciate you all. I want to sincerely thank my family and friends, especially my children, and the people who surround me on a daily basis at home and at work, for their immeasurable support. I'm grateful to my management teams and the board of directors of all of our business companies and philanthropic organizations, as well as my partners, advisors, and employees, particularly those who helped me with this book (you know who you are).

Thank you to my literary agent, Bill Gladstone of Waterside Productions, for asking me to write a second book and for his support throughout the process. Thank you very much to the editorial and promotional teams at Hay House. I am indebted

Activate Your Goodness

to Noa Mannheim, who dedicated so much time and professional assistance to help me edit my first book, *Birth: When the Spiritual and the Material Come Together,* and the original draft of this manuscript. I am also grateful to Simone Graham, who served as my editor and advisor to get *Activate Your Goodness* ready for publication.

◊   ◊   ◊

ABOUT THE AUTHOR

Shari Arison is the American-Israeli leader of a business and philanthropic empire that spans the globe. In 2010, she received the America-Israel Friendship League's Partners for Democracy Award in recognition of her contribution to advancing economic relations between the United States and Israel. In 2011, and again in 2012, she was ranked by *Forbes* magazine as one of the World's Most

Activate Your Goodness

Powerful Women, positioning her as a force for good in business and philanthropy. She was also ranked second on *Forbes*'s list of the World's Greenest Billionaires. *Activate Your Goodness* is a natural complement to her international bestseller, *Birth: When the Spiritual and the Material Come Together*. Shari is the mother of four and resides in Israel.

Please visit Shari's website at: **www.shari arison.com**. For more information on Good Deeds Day, go to: **www.good-deeds-day.org**.

◊   ◊   ◊

NOTES

NOTES

NOTES

NOTES

NOTES

Hay House Titles of Related Interest

YOU CAN HEAL YOUR LIFE, the movie,
starring Louise L. Hay & Friends
(available as a 1-DVD program and
an expanded 2-DVD set)
Watch the trailer at: **www.LouiseHayMovie.com**

THE SHIFT, the movie,
starring Dr. Wayne W. Dyer
(available as a 1-DVD program and
an expanded 2-DVD set)
Watch the trailer at: **www.DyerMovie.com**

◆ ◆ ◆

I BELIEVE: When What You Believe Matters!, by Eldon Taylor

INSPIRED DESTINY: Living a Fulfilling and Purposeful Life,
by Dr. John F. Demartini

THE POWER OF INFINITE LOVE & GRATITUDE:
An Evolutionary Journey to Awakening Your Spirit,
by Dr. Darren R. Weissman

SHIFT HAPPENS! How to Live an Inspired Life . . .
Starting Right Now!, by Robert Holden, Ph.D.

WHAT IS YOUR SELF-WORTH? A Woman's
Guide to Validation, by Cheryl Saban

WISHES FULFILLED: Mastering the Art
of Manifesting, by Dr. Wayne W. Dyer

YOU CAN CREATE AN EXCEPTIONAL LIFE,
by Louise Hay and Cheryl Richardson

All of the above are available at your local bookstore,
or may be ordered by contacting Hay House (see next page).

We hope you enjoyed this Hay House book. If you'd like
to receive our online catalog featuring additional information
on Hay House books and products, or if you'd like to find
out more about the Hay Foundation, please contact:

Hay House, Inc., P.O. Box 5100, Carlsbad, CA 92018-5100
(760) 431-7695 or (800) 654-5126
(760) 431-6948 (fax) or (800) 650-5115 (fax)
www.hayhouse.com® • **www.hayfoundation.org**

⬧ ⬧ ⬧

Published and distributed in Australia by: Hay House Australia
Pty. Ltd., 18/36 Ralph St., Alexandria NSW 2015 • *Phone:*
612-9669-4299 • *Fax:* 612-9669-4144 • www.hayhouse.com.au

Published and distributed in the United Kingdom by: Hay House
UK, Ltd., 292B Kensal Rd., London W10 5BE • *Phone:* 44-20-8962-
1230 • *Fax:* 44-20-8962-1239 • www.hayhouse.co.uk

Published and distributed in the Republic of South Africa by:
Hay House SA (Pty), Ltd., P.O. Box 990, Witkoppen 2068
Phone/Fax: 27-11-467-8904 • www.hayhouse.co.za

Published in India by: Hay House Publishers India, Muskaan
Complex, Plot No. 3, B-2, Vasant Kunj, New Delhi 110 070 • *Phone:*
91-11-4176-1620 • *Fax:* 91-11-4176-1630 • www.hayhouse.co.in

Distributed in Canada by: Raincoast,
9050 Shaughnessy St., Vancouver, B.C. V6P 6E5
Phone: (604) 323-7100 • *Fax:* (604) 323-2600 • www.raincoast.com

⬧ ⬧ ⬧

Take Your Soul on a Vacation

Visit **www.HealYourLife.com®** to regroup, recharge, and
reconnect with your own magnificence.

Featuring blogs, mind-body-spirit news, and life-changing
wisdom from Louise Hay and friends.

Visit **www.HealYourLife.com** today!

Free e-newsletters from Hay House, the Ultimate Resource for Inspiration

Be the first to know about Hay House's dollar deals, free downloads, special offers, affirmation cards, giveaways, contests, and more!

Get exclusive excerpts from our latest releases and videos from *Hay House Present Moments*.

Enjoy uplifting personal stories, how-to articles, and healing advice, along with videos and empowering quotes, within *Heal Your Life*.

Have an inspirational story to tell and a passion for writing? Sharpen your writing skills with insider tips from *Your Writing Life*.

Sign Up Now!

Get inspired, educate yourself, get a complimentary gift, and share the wisdom!

http://www.hayhouse.com/newsletters.php

Visit www.hayhouse.com to sign up today!

HAYHOUSE
RADIO
radio for your soul

HealYourLife.com

Heal Your Life One Thought at a Time . . . on Louise's All-New Website!

"Life is bringing me everything I need and more."

— Louise Hay

Come to HEALYOURLIFE.COM today and meet the world's best-selling self-help authors; the most popular leading intuitive, health, and success experts; up-and-coming inspirational writers; and new like-minded friends who will share their insights, experiences, personal stories, and wisdom so you can heal your life and the world around you . . . one thought at a time.

Here are just some of the things you'll get at HealYourLife.com:

- DAILY AFFIRMATIONS
- CAPTIVATING VIDEO CLIPS
- EXCLUSIVE BOOK REVIEWS
- AUTHOR BLOGS
- LIVE TWITTER AND FACEBOOK FEEDS
- BEHIND-THE-SCENES SCOOPS
- LIVE STREAMING RADIO
- "MY LIFE" COMMUNITY OF FRIENDS

PLUS:
FREE Monthly Contests and Polls
FREE BONUS gifts, discounts,
and newsletters

Make It Your Home Page Today!

www.HealYourLife.com®

HEAL YOUR LIFE®

051980085

CHASE BRANCH LIBRARY
17731 W. SEVEN MILE RD.
DETROIT, MI 48235
578-8002